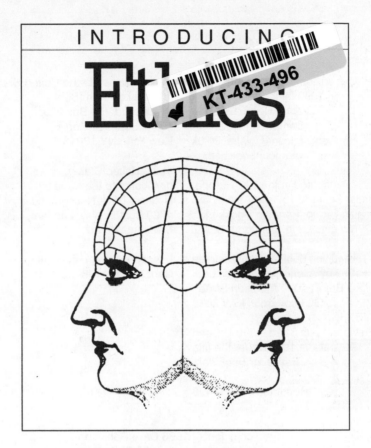

INTRODUCING

Ethics

KT-433-496

Dave Robinson and Chris Garratt

Edited by Richard Appignanesi

ICON BOOKS UK   TOTEM BOOKS USA

This edition published in the UK in 1999 by Icon Books Ltd., Grange Road, Duxford, Cambridge CB2 4QF email: icon@mistral.co.uk www.iconbooks.co.uk

First published in the United States in 1997 by Totem Books Inquiries to: PO Box 223, Canal Street Station, New York, NY 10013

Distributed in the UK, Europe, Canada, South Africa and Asia by the Penguin Group: Penguin Books Ltd., 27 Wrights Lane, London W8 5TZ

In the United States, distributed to the trade by National Book Network Inc., 4720 Boston Way, Lanham, Maryland 20706

This edition published in Australia in 1999 by Allen & Unwin Pty. Ltd., PO Box 8500, 9 Atchison Street, St. Leonards NSW 2065

Library of Congress Catalog Card Number: 96–061108

Previously published in the UK and Australia in 1996 under the title *Ethics for Beginners*

Reprinted 1997, 1998

Originating editor: Richard Appignanesi

Printed and bound in Australia by McPherson's Printing Group, Victoria

Moral Questions

Everyone is interested in ethics. We all have our own ideas about
what is right and what is wrong and how we can tell the difference.
Philosophers and bishops discuss moral "mazes" on the radio.
People no longer behave as they should.

So we're told. But there have always been "moral panics". Plato
thought 4th century B.C. Athens was doomed because of the wicked
ethical scepticism of the Sophist philosophers and the credulity of his
fellow citizens.

Social Beings

We are all products of particular societies. We do not "make ourselves". We owe much of what we consider to be our "identity" and "personal opinions" to the community in which we live. This made perfect sense to Aristotle. For Aristotle, the primary function of the state was to enable collectivist human beings to have philosophical discussions and eventually agree on a shared code of ethics.

MAN IS BY NATURE A POLITICAL ANIMAL. IT IS IN HIS NATURE TO LIVE IN A STATE.

But as soon as we are formed, most of us start to question the society that has made us, and do so in a way that seems unique to us. Socrates stressed that it was in fact our duty.

ASK **QUESTIONS** ABOUT ACCEPTED MORAL OPINIONS, AND **NEVER STOP** DOING SO.

The State may decide what is legally right and wrong, but the **law** and **morality** are not the same thing.

4

Communitarians or Individualists?

Ethics is complicated because our morality is an odd mixture of received tradition and personal opinion.

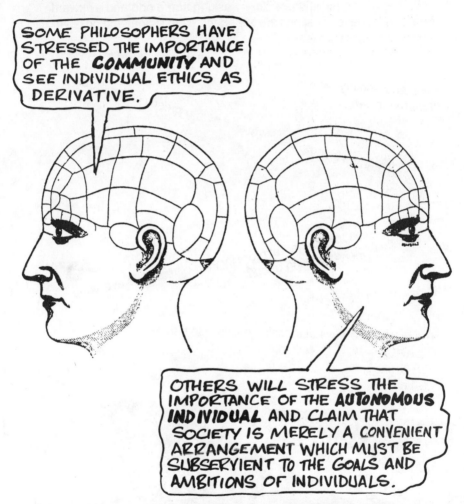

SOME PHILOSOPHERS HAVE STRESSED THE IMPORTANCE OF THE **COMMUNITY** AND SEE INDIVIDUAL ETHICS AS DERIVATIVE.

OTHERS WILL STRESS THE IMPORTANCE OF THE **AUTONOMOUS INDIVIDUAL** AND CLAIM THAT SOCIETY IS MERELY A CONVENIENT ARRANGEMENT WHICH MUST BE SUBSERVIENT TO THE GOALS AND AMBITIONS OF INDIVIDUALS.

Both **individualist** and **communitarian** philosophers are reluctant to explain away ethics as no more than "club rules" agreed upon and formalized by members. Both want to legitimize either communal ethics or the need for an individual morality by appealing to some kind of "neutral" set of ideals. Much of this book is about these different attempts to provide a foundation for ethics.

5

Setting the Stage

Ten Central Questions

Let's begin, as philosophers do, by asking some odd and awkward questions. These questions are important, even if clear and positive answers to them are few.

Are there any differences between moral laws and society's laws?
If there are, why is this?

What are human beings really like: selfish and greedy or generous and kind?

Are some people "better" at morality than others, or is everyone equally capable of being good?

Are there good ways of teaching children to behave morally?

Does anyone have the right to tell anyone else what goodness and wickedness are?

Are there certain kinds of acts (like torturing children) that are always wrong? If so, what are they?

What do you think is the best answer to the question, "Why should I be a good person?"

Is ethics a special kind of knowledge? If so, what sort of knowledge is it and how do we get hold of it?

Is morality about obeying a set of rules or is it about thinking carefully about consequences?

When people say "I know murder is wrong", do they know it is wrong or just believe it very strongly?

'Vegeta— pa

ase raises doubts over doctors'
bility to diagnose 'brain deaths'

e Dyer
l Correspondent

MAN who for seven
years was thought to
be in the same per-
manent unconscious
e as the "right to die"
lsborough victim, Tony
land, has become aware of
his surroundings and is com-
municating with hospital
staff.

At one time the health au-

the north of England dis-
cussed asking the High Court
to sanction the withdrawal of
the artificial feeding keeping
him alive. But his wife was
implacably opposed and the
idea was not pursued, al-
though relatives have no
right legally to veto doctors'
decisions in such cases.

The case of the former busi-
nessman, diagnosed as in a
persistent vegetative state
(PVS), puts a huge question
mark over —

and rais
about saf
against m
die cases.

This we
musician
tal, who h
nosed as
via a con
how he wa
night trai
ago.

The bus
much mor
cause of th
was thoug
scious, aft
error du
operation.

The Social Origins of Belief Systems

It seems very unlikely that any society has ever existed in which individual members have thought the murder of others to be acceptable. Although the odd serial killer does occasionally surface in any society, most of us think of one as an exceptional aberration, or even as "non-human".

There have always been rules about when men may kill other men – usually outsiders as opposed to insiders.

Such moral understandings are often codified and regulated by religious and legal taboos of various kinds. Human beings seem reluctant to accept that morality is something invented by themselves and so tend to legitimize moral rules by mythologizing their origins: "The Great White Parrot says stealing is wrong". The story of ethics is to some extent a description of attempts like these to legitimize morality.

Morality and Religion

Most people living in Western Christian societies would say that they base their ethical beliefs and behaviour on the ten negative commandments, rather inconveniently carved on stone tablets handed to Moses by God. (Of the ten, only about six are actually **ethical**.)

This "reciprocity rule" has a long track record and is found in many different religions worldwide. It is a bit like prudent insurance – a sensible way of getting along in the world, even if it's not quite what Jesus Christ says. (His moral code is much more radical and not at all "reciprocal". You have to do good deeds to those who have done you no good at all. This is why real Christianity is a hard act to follow.)

Is religion where morality comes from? Is being moral simply a matter of obeying divine commands? Independently-minded individuals, like Socrates (in Plato's **Euthyphro**), said that there is more to morality than religious obedience. One reason for this is that religious commands vary from one religion to another.

YOU CAN HAVE **FOUR** WIVES IF YOU FOLLOW **THIS** RELIGION, AND ONLY **ONE** IF YOU FOLLOW **THAT** ONE...

THE MORAL COMMANDS OF CHRISTIANITY OFTEN SEEM CONTRADICTORY...

...THE GOD OF THE OLD TESTAMENT SEEMS PROFOUNDLY ANTI-GAY AND HARDLY **PLURALIST**...

TOO **RIGHT**, PAL! THOU SHALT HAVE NO OTHER GODS BEFORE ME.... ...FOR I THE LORD THY GOD AM A JEALOUS GOD...

Atheists and agnostics would refuse to obey any order from God they believed to be wrong. Religion on its own doesn't seem to be a complete and satisfactory foundation for human ethical beliefs. What many philosophers search for is a way of justifying moral values which are independent of religious belief.

Morality and Human Nature

One alternative answer is to say that morality comes not from
external supernatural sources but from ourselves. This raises one
of the **big questions** of **all time**.

Thinking on ethics often begins with assumptions about human
nature, either negative or positive. For instance, the Christian notion of
"original sin" takes the view that our nature is "fallen" and essentially
bad. If this is the case, then it is our social environment and its legal
sanctions that force us all to be moral. But the reason most of us don't
torture children is because we think it is **wrong**, not because we fear a
visit from the police.

This negative Christian verdict is an example of the "programmed" view of human nature. There is an opposite "Romantic" view of human nature which assumes it to be positively programmed for good.

Men may kill other men in different uniforms because society encourages them to do so, but their genetic instincts might be to do things like play football and drink beer with each other.

Genetics

Nowadays, arguments about human nature centre more and more on genetics. Words like "selfish gene" and "altruistic gene" turn up in popular science articles, but no-one is sure yet what these terms mean or what the full implications of them are. Geneticists use the word "selfish" in an odd sort of way, so that many people now assume erroneously that it is possible to identify "criminality" from DNA. Genetics is an empirical science, but the subsequent arguments and discussions about "human nature" that new genetic "facts" stimulate are full of political myths, ideological assertions and dangerous tosh.

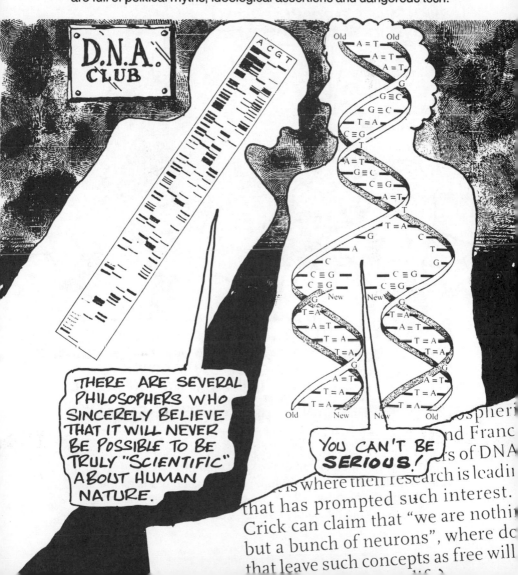

...spheri...
...nd Franc...
...rs of DNA
...rch is leadi...
...s where then research is leading...
that has prompted such interest.
Crick can claim that "we are nothin...
but a bunch of neurons", where d...
that leave such concepts as free will

The whole debate is highly speculative and unscientific. Worse, it may be what philosophers call a form of **"language bewitchment"**. We assume that because there are convenient human terms like "good" and "bad" and "human nature" that there are real physical concrete entities to which these words refer. They very probably don't exist as "genes" at all. Geneticists prefer words like "potential", "propensity" and "encourage" rather than "cause" or "determine".

ONE GENE MAY GIVE SOMEONE A PROPENSITY FOR **VERTIGO** WHICH MIGHT ENCOURAGE THEM TO LIVE IN FLAT AREAS.

BUT IT DIDN'T STOP **ME** FROM BECOMING A MOUNTAIN CLIMBER. THE SOCIAL AND CULTURAL INFLUENCES IN MY CHILDHOOD WERE STRONG ENOUGH AND I HAD **WILL POWER**.

Talk about genes means that the old and eternally unsolveable debate about "nature versus nurture" crops up and drags all the usual political baggage along with it. Those who wish to preserve political power structures are often very keen on **genetic determinism**.

14

Do We Have Any Choice?

Some philosophers maintain that DNA and social environment have little or no influence on the sorts of people we become and the moral choices that we make. We are almost wholly autonomous individuals who make our own moral decisions in life and therefore we alone are responsible for all the good and bad things that we do. After all, without free will, we are little more than robots and cannot be moral beings at all. It is a commonplace in ethics that **"ought implies can"**. You can't even begin to talk about morality, unless you assume that human beings have freedom to choose.

IT JUST ISN'T SENSIBLE TO CALL CATS "WICKED" WHEN THEY KILL MICE.

BUT WE **DO** THINK THAT HITLER AND CHARLES MANSON WERE RIGHTLY PUNISHED FOR **THEIR** WICKED BEHAVIOUR.

THEIR GENETIC MAKE-UP AND EARLY SOCIAL ENVIRONMENT ARE NOT GOOD ENOUGH EXCUSES FOR WHAT THEY DID.

Nevertheless, "commonsense" views like these can be naive or prejudiced. A brutal society can often have a strong negative influence on the formation of someone's moral character.

Is Society to Blame?

Even if DNA has little or no influence on our moral character, perhaps we are still products of our social and cultural environment. At birth, we are blank sheets of paper that are gradually written on by parents, teachers, peer groups, the media and all sorts of other ideological forces. The influence of society on our moral personalities is infinitely stronger than any genetic inheritance and almost totally responsible for everything that makes us both human and moral. This means that it is nonsense to talk about some absurd fiction like "human nature", as if it has some kind of pre-societal existence. This view is held by many sociologists:

THERE IS NO SUCH THING AS INNATE "HUMAN NATURE" —ONLY CITIZENS INTERNALIZING EXTERNAL MORAL CODES.

IT IS ALSO A VIEW HELD BY MANY MARXISTS WHO BELIEVE WE ARE MERELY PRODUCTS OF THE IDEOLOGIES OF THE DOMINANT CLASS.

IF I AM BAD (OR GOOD), THEN SOCIETY IS TO BLAME, RIGHT?

Human nature might either be wholly **plastic**, and subsequently given "ethical shape" by social forces, or a **programmed** bundle of moral software. What puzzles philosophers is the variation in ethical beliefs held by different societies at different times.

Moral Relativism

The recognition of this wide variety of ethical beliefs and practices is usually called **moral relativism**. Differences in moral belief exist between different countries and tribes, but can also exist between different subcultures within a society, or between different classes. History also demonstrates how time alters moral beliefs.

MOST 20TH CENTURY WESTERNERS WOULD BE HORRIFIED BY THE IDEA OF PUBLIC EXECUTIONS AS ENTERTAINMENT...

..BUT MOST MEDIEVAL EUROPEANS WOULD BE APPALLED BY THE IDEA OF NUCLEAR BOMBS.

Nowadays there are very different sets of moral beliefs held by feminists and religious fundamentalists about abortion.

FOR SOME, IT'S A WOMAN'S RIGHT TO CHOOSE...

...FOR OTHERS, IT'S MURDER.

Ethical Absolutism

If there are all of these moral beliefs floating around, which one is right? How could we prove that one belief was right and others wrong? Most ethical relativists would say that there are no possible ways of deciding, and no such thing as moral "knowledge" at all. This kind of scepticism has worried other philosophers who think that there must surely be a set of universal moral rules that are always true. These philosophers are often called **"Universalists"**, **"Realists"** or **"Absolutists"**.

UNIVERSALISTS SAY THAT THERE ARE UNIVERSAL MORAL RULES.

ABSOLUTISTS CLAIM THAT THEY ARE ALWAYS COMPULSORY.

REALISTS SAY THAT THE RULES ARE A TRUE KIND OF KNOWLEDGE.

All three would say that it was always wrong to sacrifice babies, regardless of the beliefs of the culture that encouraged or allowed this practice.

The danger of **Ethical Absolutism** is that it can legitimize one powerful culture imposing its own local moral values on all others, by claiming a monopoly on the moral "truth".

WESTERN MISSIONARIES ONCE RUSHED OUT INTO THE WORLD WITH BIBLES AND BRASSIÈRES TO CONVERT THE "HEATHEN."

TODAY, ADVOCATES OF ETHICAL RELATIVISM ACTUALLY WELCOME AND CELEBRATE DIFFERENCES BETWEEN CULTURES AND ARE CRITICAL OF THE NAIVE ARROGANCE OF EUROCENTRIC "MORAL IMPERIALISM."

Westerners have also been witness to, and a cause of, the wholesale destruction of hundreds of unique cultures with their own ethical beliefs. Now we make some inadequate attempts to protect "innocent" and "primitive" tribal cultures and wring our hands in shame when we hear of their annihilation. We send out anthropologists and leave our Bibles and underwear at home.

Relativism versus Absolutism

Now most Western liberals and academics would not interfere with the moral beliefs and customs of other cultures.

An ethical absolutist would then smile rather smugly and get us to admit that perhaps there are a few universal moral rules that are always true, wherever you are, like:

Another Absolutist Reply

Some societies may look as if they go in for weird immoral behaviour, different from our own, but there seem to be a few fundamental core values like "Murder is wrong" that are always followed. A tribe may burn widows and sacrifice children in the belief that this is for the ultimate long-term heavenly good of the victims involved, but they don't sanction the murder of widows and children as such. Absolutists say that Relativists only look at what people do, not at what they actually **believe**.

ALSO, THE EXISTENCE OF A WIDE VARIETY OF MORAL BELIEFS DOESN'T PROVE THAT ALL MORAL BELIEFS ARE EQUALLY VALID.

DARK CONTINENT

DIFFERENT PEOPLE ONCE HELD VERY DIFFERENT BELIEFS ABOUT THE SHAPE OF THE EARTH.

NOT ALL THESE BELIEFS WERE "VALID" — ONLY ONE SET OF "ROUND EARTHERS" ACTUALLY KNEW THE TRUTH.

DONUT-SHAPED EARTH

NORTH HOLE

Absolutists say that human morality is like this — there is real "moral knowledge". Some moral beliefs are "true" and some aren't, it's just that we haven't figured out how to prove which is which yet.

Are They Both Wrong?

Although the differences between Relativists and Absolutists are clear enough, they both face certain problems. Absolutists have to explain what the "core" moral rules are, and why they've selected the ones they have. Absolutists claim that the core moral rules are generally those "foundational" ones that enable societies to exist. But there can be problems with this definition of core values.

FEW ABSOLUTISTS WOULD HAVE ADMIRED NAZI GERMANY WITH ITS VERY CLEAR AND COHESIVE SOCIAL "RULES", AND

MANY RELATIVISTS WOULD NO DOUBT HAVE APPLAUDED THE WAY IN WHICH THE ALLIES INTERFERED RATHER DRASTICALLY WITH FASCIST VALUES IN THE SECOND WORLD WAR.

Yet most Relativists also believe in one absolute moral rule: "Don't interfere with other cultures".

The Problem of Moral Knowledge

The main difference between Relativists and Absolutists lies in their disagreement about the possibility of moral beliefs ever becoming true or proven. Relativists are often "subjectivists" who say that moral beliefs are really no more than subjective feelings about behaviour which can never achieve the status of facts.

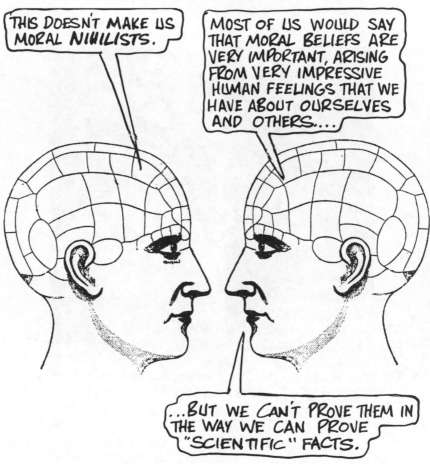

It is now time that we surveyed the history of ethical beliefs. We will limit ourselves to Western ideas, beginning with the Ancient Greeks, although many of the positions expressed could equally well be found in other non-Western cultures.

A Brief History of Ethics

The Greek City State

One of the most impressive examples of group living was the Greek City State or *Polis* of Athens in the 5th century B.C. This City State wasn't exactly tribal or like a modern State but something in between. City States were small and Athens was the most famous because sometimes it was "democratic". The Athens *Polis* was about the size of Dorset (1000 square miles) with a population of around 250,000.

Aristotle would have been horrified by modern states in which vast populations have almost no say in how things are run.

Democracy

Only adult males over eighteen could become Athenian citizens, and being one was a very serious business which involved duties as well as privileges. Athens ran its affairs by calling an Assembly which met regularly to pass laws and decide upon government policy. The Athenians realized how important it was to be ruled by law and not by the arbitrary whims of kings or priests. It's hard for us modern "citizens" to get our heads around what this actually means.

Athens wasn't Utopian. Women and slaves had no political say and, as is usually the case, the rich and powerful still got to be policy-makers and had more influence than ordinary citizens. Nevertheless, Athenians invented some astounding ideas – like the right to vote and have a fair trial.

Greeks and Philosophy

The Greeks were not only inventors of democracy, theatre, pure mathematics and much else, but also of a new kind of thinking, now called "philosophical".

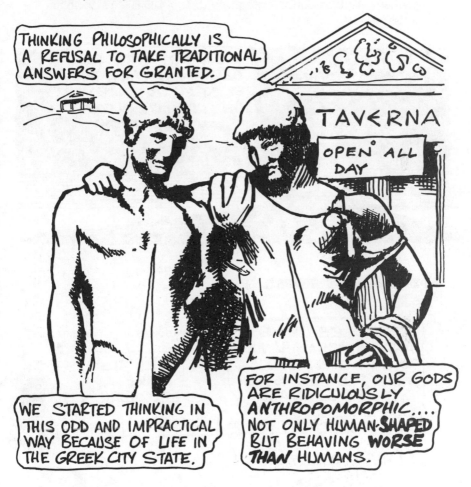

Their gods were immortal, violent, randy and politically incorrect. They often recommended that their mortal subjects went to war. They fell in and out of love and quarrelled with each other all the time. They seduced and impregnated human mortals, often in very peculiar costumes and circumstances.

For thinkers like Socrates, the Gods must have been exceedingly inadequate as moral role models. There were no "Ten Commandments" to follow from Greek mythology. So, although most Greek intellectuals like Socrates paid lip service to the usual religious ceremonies and rituals required of them, they didn't take religion very seriously. Some philosophers, like the Sophist **Protagoras** (c.490-420 B.C.) said about the Gods:

And **Xenophanes** (c. 570-475 B.C.) said:

This means that ethics had to be sought for outside of religion.

Slavery

Although many Athenians had to work hard, higher-class Athenian men did no work at all. There were probably about 80,000 slaves in Athens – some working in appalling conditions in the silver mines, many employed as domestics. Greek philosophers owned slaves. Plato mentions five in his will and Aristotle seems to have had about fourteen. The institution of slavery never seems to have worried these moral philosophers at all. Aristotle seems to have sincerely believed that some people are slaves "by nature". The institution of slavery also meant that Greek technology was very primitive. No one, for example, thought of transferring the simple technology of the sailing boat to the windmill...

Philosophy was a communal activity, not a solitary pursuit. This is why Plato actually distrusted the new invention of books – they are closed systems of one individual and can never be corrected.

The Socratic Method

Socrates (c. 469-399 B.C.) was a stonemason's son and fat, bow-legged, bald, snub-nosed and scruffy. His nickname was "the Gadfly" because he would sting people into thinking clearly for themselves. He was condemned to death in 399 B.C. by the democratic government of Athens because he refused to recognize the Gods.

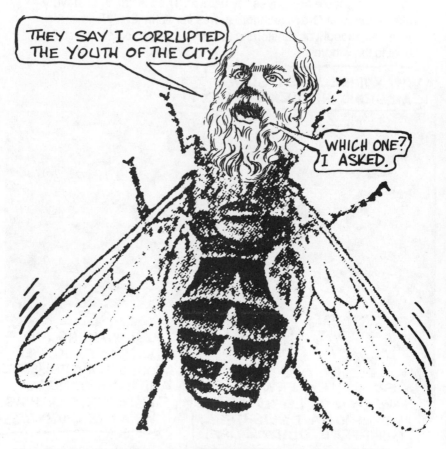

He was never dogmatic or authoritarian, but for many young people he seems to have been some sort of guru.

Socrates believed that the most important thing about human beings is that they ask questions. He also said that real moral knowledge existed and was worth pursuing for its own sake.

According to Socrates, "the unexamined life is not worth living". It's a disturbing idea. Questions about one's moral life are avoided by most adults – they prefer to earn money and live lives of undisturbed routine. The Gadfly encouraged young people to think for themselves and question all the usual adult moral rules. Socrates didn't want to be a guru handing down "wisdom".

He usually began by puzzling people with questions like "What is Right Behaviour?", or "What is a State?", subsequently revealing how little people knew about either morality or politics. He always stressed that the wise man is **"he who knows that he knows nothing"**. Socrates perfected a method of enquiry that philosophers are now rather proud of.

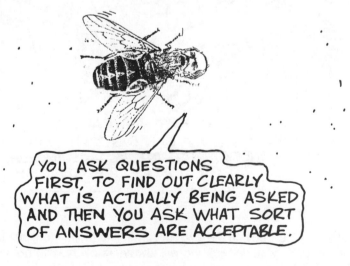

Socratic Ethics: Know Thyself

Socrates had some moral beliefs. Like most Greeks, he thought that human beings are like manufactured objects in that they have a purpose or function (sometimes called the **teleological** view). We are pre-programmed with "software" and it is our job to discover what the codes are and carry them out correctly.

Morality isn't just obeying the law, but something much more spiritual. Once we know who we are, we will always know how to behave well.

Although moral knowledge is reachable through debate and discussion, Socrates stresses that morality is not the sort of knowledge that you can actually be taught. Real knowledge is about "essences" of things, like "Right Behaviour" or "Justice", that ultimately you have to discover for yourself.

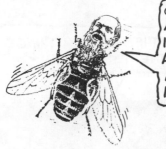

ONCE YOU HAVE THIS KNOWLEDGE AND YOUR "INNER EYE" CAN SEE IT ALL CLEARLY, THEN YOU WILL ALWAYS KNOW WHAT IS RIGHT, AND AS A RESULT YOU WILL NEVER BE WICKED.

This is what Socrates means by phrases like "Virtue is knowledge" and "No one does wrong knowingly". The Athenian Democrats thought this was dangerous stuff.

SOCRATES ENCOURAGES YOUNG PEOPLE TO QUESTION CONVENTIONAL STATE MORALITY!

HE URGES THEM TO CHOOSE A VERY DIFFERENT ONE, BASED ON A PERSONAL VISION OF SPIRITUAL PERFECTION!

Socrates certainly got moral philosophy started, but he caused many subsequent philosophers a lot of headaches.

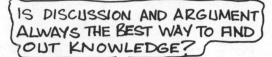

IS DISCUSSION AND ARGUMENT ALWAYS THE BEST WAY TO FIND OUT KNOWLEDGE?

ARE THERE SUCH THINGS AS THE "ESSENCES"?

DO WE HAVE A "REAL" INNER SELF" OR "FUNCTION" AND HOW WOULD WE KNOW WHEN WE HAD DISCOVERED IT?

IS MORALITY A KIND OF KNOWLEDGE LIKE GEOGRAPHY OR IS IT MORE LIKE MATHEMATICS?

IS IT A KIND OF KNOWLEDGE AT **ALL**?

HAS ANYONE GOT AN ASPIRIN?

Socrates tends to envisage morality as a kind of self-discovery, but isn't morality more about our relationships with other people and taking responsibility for our actions? Once we know what is right, we will never do wrong, says Socrates. But what about all those people who know what they are doing is wrong but still choose to do wrong? What about people who are just too weak-willed or wicked to do the right thing? Don't you have to **choose** to do the right thing as well as **know** what it is?

Plato's Republic

Socrates' most famous student was a young aristocrat called **Plato** (c. 428-354 B.C.) who never forgave the Athenian Democrats for murdering his teacher. Democracy for Plato meant chaos and rule by a violent and ignorant mob easily swayed by corrupt politicians. He left Athens in disgust, but later returned to find his City State in deep trouble.

Athens had been defeated by Sparta in 405 B.C. The citizens were discontented and Sophist philosophers like **Thrasymachus** were spreading rumours that there was no such thing as morality. Plato's great work **The Republic** is an extraordinary book because it raises nearly every philosophical question there is. **A.N. Whitehead** once said that all of Western philosophy is really no more than "footnotes" to Plato.

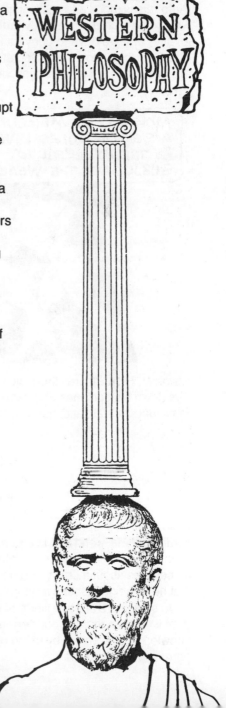

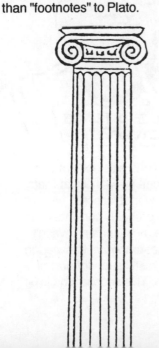

Plato versus the Sophists

Plato raises moral and political questions about the State itself –
why being a citizen is as inevitable as breathing, why it demands
loyalty, why we have to obey its laws, and why it is a good thing.
The Republic begins with Socratic open dialogue – several Sophists
are allowed to put forward their views about law and morality.

MORALITY IS MERELY A SET OF RULES INVENTED BY THE POWERFUL TO SUBJUGATE THE WEAK.

MORALITY IS JUST A SOCIAL CONTRACT.

However, Plato ignores them all and
lays down his doctrines about the
individual, the state and morality.

THERE'S A PLACE SOMEWHERE....

Plato is a "Two Worlder". He believes both in the existence of this
sordid material world and in a purer, better one as well. What Plato
says about our knowledge of both of these worlds accords with what
he believes about morality and politics. This probably convinced him
that he was right about everything, when he most certainly wasn't.
Plato says there are two kinds of knowledge: **empirical** knowledge
(that we obtain through our **senses**) and a vastly superior sort of
knowledge that we get by using our **reason**. This second kind is
permanent and eternal.

Virtually everyone can get access to empirical knowledge because most of us have five working senses. Only a very few experts can ever discover "real" knowledge, because you need very specially developed ability and training to "see" it mentally. Plato is a **Rationalist** – a philosopher who believes that real knowledge has to come from reason.

> THE PHYSICAL WORLD THAT WE EXPERIENCE EVERY DAY IS ONE OF "HALF-REAL" SHADOWS! KNOWLEDGE OF THIS WORLD IS JUST THIRD RATE "OPINION."

One source of this belief is mathematics. All Greek intellectuals were stunned by the beauty, permanence and purity of mathematics.

Numbers do not exist in the real world but somehow both in your head and in some other abstract, perhaps spiritual, place. Plato thought all knowledge could be as permanent and unchanging as mathematics.

The World of Forms

Plato says that the everyday world of the senses is surpassed by an extraordinary and incredible world of "**Forms**". The Forms are permanent, timeless and "real". The Forms explain how we know a red apple when we see one – because it shares the Forms of "Apple" and "Red". The Forms in this perfect world are of everything from "The Perfect Chair" to "Beauty", "Goodness" and "The Perfect State".

The political conclusion to all this is that perfect infallible knowledge is something that only a few individual specialists can ever possess. Plato says that these specialists must be put in charge of everybody else. The "Guardians" will always know the correct answers to any problem and know what to do.

A Closed Society

Plato was a moral absolutist who thought that moral knowledge was "coded" in the universe, as some mathematicians think that numbers are coded. But are there moral "facts", like facts about giraffes or triangles? Ethical absolutism like this assumes a bureaucratic model of what morality should be like – a special knowledge known only by experts.

WE HAVE TO **ASK** WHAT TO DO.

THERE ARE NO RULES LAID DOWN.

Plato assumes that the morality of the individual and the morality of the State are the same thing. This could lead to immoral repressive tyrannies ruled by self-declared "élites" who judge individuals solely on how well they contribute to the State. Many people in this century have had very unpleasant experiences of closed societies ruled by self-perpetuating élites in charge of centralized monolithic truths.

PLATO HAS FORGOTTEN THAT ARGUMENT AND DEBATE, AND LOTS OF DIFFERENT POLITICAL VIEWS, ARE GOOD THINGS IN THEMSELVES!

Aristotle and Commonsense Ethics

Aristotle (384-322 B.C.) was Plato's student and came from northern Greece. Aristotle became the tutor of Alexander the Great (also from the north) and eventually founded his own university – the Lyceum. He agreed with Plato that humans are essentially social beings, best organized in City States. But as far as morality is concerned, Aristotle is more pragmatic.

ETHICS IS A ROUGH'N'READY SORT OF BUSINESS THAT HAS TO BE DETERMINED BY ORDINARY PRACTICAL MEN OF COMMON SENSE, NOT BY INBRED ASCETIC "EXPERTS" WITH THEIR HEADS IN THE REMOTE AND AUSTERE WORLD OF "FORMS".

LYCEVM

PHILOSOPHY + SCIENCES + BALLROOM DANCING
★ ★ ★ ★ DRESS : SMART CASUAL ★ ★ ★ ★

Aristotle is more interested in what ordinary people think about morality on a day-to-day basis.

The Teleological View and the "Mean"

In **The Nichomachean Ethics**, Aristotle stresses that he is not interested in remote abstractions, like "Goodness itself", but in ordinary everyday goodness that most people choose most of the time.
The driving force behind virtually all of Aristotle's philosophy is the belief that the ultimate meaning of all things can be understood from an examination of their different ends.

EVERYTHING IS HEADING TOWARDS ITS OWN UNIQUE PERFECT DESTINY. JUST AS A KNIFE FULFILS ITS PURPOSE BY CUTTING WELL, HUMAN BEINGS ARE FULFILLED AND HAPPY WHEN THEY'RE FUNCTIONING WELL.

It's as if we are already programmed with the "moral software" of justice, fairness, temperance, courage and so on, but it's up to us to realize its full potential. Sensible people do this by choosing a **"mean"** between extremes. As good humans, we should try to be reasonably courageous, but not ridiculously reckless or absurdly timid.
Aristotle is also quite clear about moral responsibility – if you choose to do something wrong, then you should be punished for it.

A Dull but Good Person

Aristotle's ideal is essentially a dull middle-aged sensible Athenian
male citizen who is calm and rational, avoids extremes, and knows
how to behave from experience. If we can be like this, he thinks, then
we will be psychologically content. We become moral by working at it,
just as we learn to play the piano by practising.

We gradually learn to choose a "mean"
which is right for us and each morally
problematic situation. When the time
comes for us to decide whether to give
just some or all of our money away to
charity, we will know what to do. And
when we have this kind of confidence
in ourselves and our moral judgement,
we'll be happy because we will have
fulfilled our destiny.

Aristotle's views on moral responsibility seem sensible enough and have been very influential in law. When you choose to steal and you get caught, then you have to take the blame. It's as simple and obvious as that. If you have been compelled to take it by threats of violence, or you took it by mistake, then you're off the hook. But what Aristotle won't allow you to do is what Socrates thought you could do.

Aristotle's views seem strange because nowadays we don't confuse morality with self-fulfilment. And are we "programmed" with certain dispositions in the way that Aristotle thinks we are? In a post-Romantic age that celebrates individualism and personal choice, many of us would also reject the idea that "good citizenship" is the ideal to aim for.

Most of Aristotle's moral doctrine also seems very dull – as careful compromise usually is. The doctrine of the Mean may make some kind of sense where courage is concerned.

BUT HOW DO YOU CHOOSE AN APPROPRIATE "MEAN" FOR TELLING THE TRUTH OR COMMITTING ADULTERY?

YOU EITHER DO OR YOU DON'T.... AN AFFABLE COMPROMISE DOESN'T SEEM POSSIBLE.

Aristotle may provide us with guidance on how to be fulfilled, but we don't get any moral rules to help us see how we should relate to others. But he may be right to suggest that morality is a very approximate "science" or skill – more like learning to drive a car than studying physics.

LEARNING TO DRIVE A CAR? IS THAT HOW YOU SEE OUR RELATIONSHIP?

Many modern moral philosophers now think that there is a great deal in what he says, of which more later.

Hellenistic Ethics

The influence of Greek thought on moral philosophy was profound, and lasted long after the City States collapsed and were exchanged for the new military empires of Alexander the Great (356-323 B.C.) and then Rome. Greek moral philosophy survived in various forms in Macedonia, Syria and Egypt, and from about 50 B.C. throughout the whole Roman Empire. "Hellenistic" moral philosophy is mostly a series of additions to Aristotle's views on human fulfilment and happiness.

The Cynics

The **Cynics**, founded by **Antisthenes** (c. 444-366 B.C.), claimed that happiness lay in cultivating an indifference to worldly ambition and possessions because the individual is never able to control these things for long. Their most colourful spokesman was **Diogenes** (d. 320 B.C.), who lived in a barrel and was rude to Alexander the Great.

Stoics and Epicureans

Both Stoics and Epicureans differ from Aristotle in one key respect: both suggest that the wise man avoids or ignores the corruption and compromise of political life. This is because they are no longer members of a democratic City State, but alienated individuals living under an impersonal and corrupt Empire.

The **Stoics**, founded by **Zeno of Citium** (c. 336-261 B.C.), believed in "Natural Law" – a doctrine that later became very important to Medieval Scholasticism. Their most famous disciples were Romans – among them the statesman and orator Cicero and the Emperor Marcus Aurelius. The Stoical view on individual lives is fatalist.

WE ARE ALL GOVERNED BY NATURAL LAW AND WE MUST ACCEPT WHAT LIFE THROWS AT US WITH CALMNESS AND COURAGE.

THE WISE MAN THEREFORE LIMITS HIS WANTS TO CLEARLY ACHIEVABLE THINGS...

ZENO

BUT LOVE IS BLIND, AND LOVERS CANNOT SEE THE PRETTY FOLLIES THAT THEMSELVES COMMIT.

The Stoics thought human passions often made human beings disastrously irrational – a view of human nature that Shakespeare seems to have shared.

The **Epicureans**, founded by **Epicurus** (341-270 B.C.), equated happiness with pleasure, something Aristotle had always been careful to avoid. However, "pleasure" for Epicureans had to be pursued with Aristotelian moderation, and came in many forms: friendship and philosophical discussion, as well as wine and song. In fact, Epicureans were more Stoical than they sound.

WE BELIEVE THAT SELF-CONTROL AND SERENITY CAN HELP MOST PEOPLE ENDURE MOST THINGS.

They were also sometimes known as the "garden philosophers" because of their belief that private individual happiness could only be achieved by escaping from public political life.

The Advent of Christianity

By the 4th century A.D., Christianity was the official religion of the whole of the Roman Empire. The Empire itself became two empires in A.D. 330 when Constantine moved the capital from Rome to Constantinople.

By A.D. 476 the western half had collapsed. In 529 the Church finally closed Plato's Academy in Athens and moral philosophy became a part of Christian theology, although the influence of Plato and Aristotle kept surfacing in the works of the Church fathers. **St. Augustine** (354-430) tried to harmonize the Gospel teachings and Plato's philosophy. He tackled a major problem for Christians.

Medieval and Scholastic Ethics

Virtually all medieval philosophers were churchmen who accepted that Christianity was true. This means that moral debate often centred on questions that seem to us now more theological and technical than "moral".

The teachings of Aristotle were assimilated by the greatest medieval theologian, **St. Thomas Aquinas** (1224-74).

Aquinas had more interesting things to say about society's laws and the individual. Laws, according to Aquinas, must be more than just a reflection of the personal whims of government. They are necessary for the common good of all and reflect "Natural Law" which is "impressed" on all of us by God. Secular law is admittedly useful because it ensures public order and makes social life possible.

The Rise of Humanism

Eventually science and philosophy started to break away from the influence and teachings of the Church, just as Greek philosophy had questioned mythology and superstition two thousand years earlier. The **Renaissance** started in northern Italy in the 14th century and spread throughout Europe in the 15th and 16th.

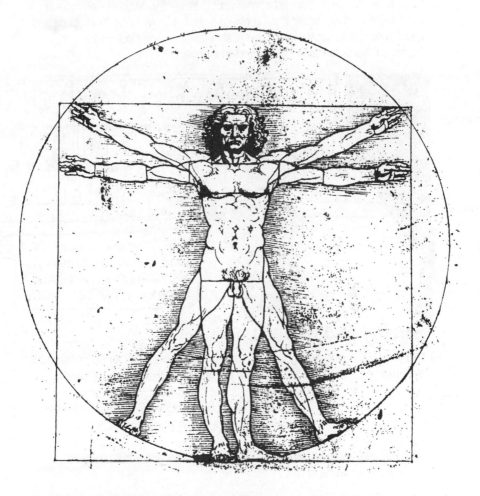

Renaissance "**Humanism**" placed greater emphasis on human achievement and less on the role of God in human affairs. It also encouraged a greater stress on the usefulness and productivity of the empirical method in science.
The **Reformation** hastened this whole process.

Machiavelli

The interest in the relationship between morality and the State
continued during the Renaissance, and its most famous writer on this
topic was **Niccolò Machiavelli**.

Machiavelli (1469-1527) was born in Florence, a City State like
Athens, although governed somewhat differently. Machiavelli was a
practical diplomat rather than a philosopher. His famous book is called
The Prince, and was one of the first ever to be placed on the
Catholic Church's Index of Forbidden Books.

Morality and Public Life

The Prince is ostensibly a technical book on politics but its subtext is
definitely ethics. What Machiavelli points out is that all good rulers
need *virtù* – the "masculine" qualities of self reliance, courage,
resoluteness and so on. However, to be a really successful ruler also
means going in for "necessary immorality". A prince must lie, betray,
cheat, steal and kill.
"It is necessary for a prince who wishes to maintain his position to
learn how not to be good..."

Machiavelli then describes some of the rather un-Christian ways in
which Cesare Borgia operated: he didn't think it was always
necessary to keep promises or tell the truth; he invited rebel soldiers to
dinner and then had them strangled; he appointed a cruel deputy to
enforce his own laws, whom he then executed.

Disagreements About the Book

Readers of Machiavelli's book have always argued over it. Some, like the Catholic Church, believed it to be a wicked book, others think it is a satire, others say it is not a moral or immoral book but a "technical" book. However, there's not much doubt that Machiavelli admired successful princes in spite of their methods. He was, like Hobbes, fairly pessimistic about human nature. He thought princes had to be immoral.

MEN WILL ALWAYS BEHAVE LIKE VILLAINS TOWARDS YOU, UNLESS THEY'RE UNDER SOME COMPULSION TO BE HONEST...

Machiavelli Today

The Prince is important, not because it offers any great philosophical insights into ethics, the individual and governments, but because of the way it has helped to establish a climate of opinion which suggests that there is inevitably a difference between private and public morality. (Sometimes associated in people's minds with "female" and "male" ethics, of which more later.) Many people today still believe that you have to be pragmatic and prudent or "unethical" in political life, business dealings and the public sphere generally. There have to be two sets of moral standards.

GREED IS GOOD.

IT'S DOG EAT DOG IN THIS BUSINESS.

MY COUNTRY RIGHT OR WRONG.

Machiavelli thought politics and morality were awkward companions.

Brutes or Innocents?

Machiavelli's influential "political science" launched a continuing debate about human nature and morality in the 17th and 18th centuries.

Are human beings brutes, tamed and dragged into becoming moral beings by society, or are they moral innocents corrupted by society? The debate is interesting because some of its conclusions about societies, individuals and the need for government are still relevant.

Thomas Hobbes (1588-1679), the 17th century English Royalist, philosopher and author of **Leviathan**, popularized the doctrine that says human nature is basically nasty. This account is often called **"Psychological Egoism"**.

HUMAN BEINGS ARE JUST INNATELY BAD AND NO ONE CAN DO MUCH ABOUT IT.

BUT IF THIS IS TRUE, — HOW ON EARTH DOES MORALITY EVER GET STARTED?

The Social Contract

Hobbes' solution is a legalistic form of the reciprocity idea, usually called "The Social Contract". Hobbes thought that morality was simply a way for wicked but rational human beings to avoid conflict. When there is no society, then human beings live in a "state of nature" where everyone's life is "solitary, poor, nasty, brutish and short".

In order to make this "social contract" enforceable, they also make a further "Government Contract" with a neutral third party who agrees to enforce the first "Social" one.

That's how societies get started and why strong and firm governments are a good idea – to save us from the results of our innate wickedness.

Is It True?

Hobbes' explanation about where morality comes from is not totally convincing. Lots of people behave very oddly for "psychological egoists" – they jump into frozen lakes to save drowning children and secretly give money to charities. Most of Hobbes' talk about a "state of nature" isn't very historical. There's little evidence for this "atomistic" theory about pre-societal murderers making "contracts".

Our nearest genetic relatives, the great apes, conduct their lives harmoniously and are a very gregarious bunch of mutual groomers. And it looks as if human beings have always been social animals living in families and tribes, not as isolated loners.

Romantic Innocence

The opposite doctrine to Hobbes' pessimistic one is sometimes known as the "Romantic" view, and really started with **Jean-Jacques Rousseau** (1712-78). Rousseau's view is that we are born as moral beings with a huge potential for goodness, and that is why children's education is so important.

WE ALL ONCE LIVED IN A STATE OF INNOCENT HARMONY WITH OUR SURROUNDINGS. THEN THE GREAT ENTERPRIZE OF **CIVILIZATION** GOT INVENTED.

This brought with it artificial needs like CD players and fast cars and corresponding vices like greed and sexual depravity. Although getting corrupted by civilized tastes sounds like fun, the result was that our innate goodness and innocence got corrupted. These are the views that Rousseau puts forward in **Discourse on the Arts and Sciences** and **Emile.**

The Noble Savage

Unlike Hobbes, Rousseau thought it possible to form a society that virtually dispensed with government through the expression of "the General Will" – a doctrine both vague and dangerous. Who is going to discover and then enforce this "Will" on people? Primordial human innocence is also a doctrine about human nature which ultimately leads to the myth of the Noble Savage – the belief that "primitive" peoples, like native Americans, lead simpler, more fulfilling and morally superior lives to decadent Westerners. It's a myth.

THERE IS NOTHING 'SIMPLE' OR ESSENTIALLY 'MORAL' ABOUT THE LIVES OF PEOPLES IN LESS TECHNOLOGICALLY DEVELOPED CULTURES.

"Noble savagery" is used to satirize the moral sins and perceived excesses of civilized society. To some extent, it led to the whole complicated "Romantic Movement" which often suggested that moral instruction best comes from trees, children and peasants rather than philosophers or politicians. In its earlier days, the Romantic Movement was also revolutionary and even anarchist in its sympathies.

ANARCHISTS NEED A BENIGN MODEL OF HUMAN NATURE IF THEY ARE TO DISPENSE WITH GOVERNMENTS AND THE NEED FOR POLICE AND PRISONS.

Mutual Aiders or Sociobiology

Peter Kropotkin (1842-1921), the anarchist philosopher, and the more recent sociobiologist **Edward O. Wilson** (b. 1929), both believe something rather less radically polarized about human nature and morality.

MORALITY HAS MORE OR LESS EVOLVED OUT OF HUMAN NATURE, WITHOUT THE NEED FOR ANY LEGALISTIC FRAMEWORKS BASED ON A **MUTUAL FEAR**.

NOR IS MORALITY SOMETHING INNATE THAT HAS LONG SINCE BEEN ANNIHILATED BY **CIVILIZATION**.

Simply by looking around us, we can see that there is an impressive amount of evidence to show that human beings are neither motivated by violent greed, nor are they corrupted innocents. Large numbers of human beings do seem to possess very real motives of friendship, loyalty, compassion, generosity and sympathy, as well as those of greed and selfishness.

Nature provides evidence of co-operation amongst animals and plants, which is how "ecosystems" come into being in the first place. Many species apart from ourselves exist in harmonious groups and raise their offspring with apparent love and affection.

If human beings are "selfish" then they are so in an oddly co-operative way, otherwise there wouldn't be families, tribes and societies.

The Social Gene

This is not to suggest that we are genetically and robotically programmed in the way that other social animals like ants and bees seem to be. Our programming is less fixed and absolute.

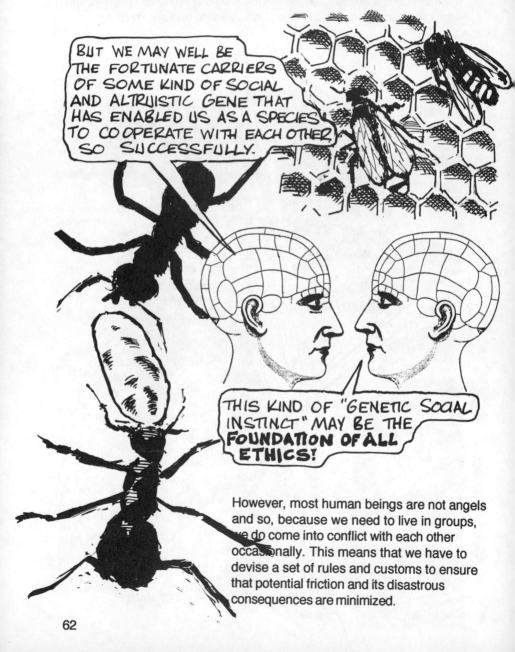

BUT WE MAY WELL BE THE FORTUNATE CARRIERS OF SOME KIND OF SOCIAL AND ALTRUISTIC GENE THAT HAS ENABLED US AS A SPECIES TO COOPERATE WITH EACH OTHER SO SUCCESSFULLY.

THIS KIND OF "GENETIC SOCIAL INSTINCT" MAY BE THE FOUNDATION OF ALL ETHICS!

However, most human beings are not angels and so, because we need to live in groups, we do come into conflict with each other occasionally. This means that we have to devise a set of rules and customs to ensure that potential friction and its disastrous consequences are minimized.

Symbolic Animals

We differ from animals by doing what we do consciously. Human beings are able to choose and take responsibility for the decisions that they make. Other animals live in a non-conscious, non-symbolic world of instinct, even though their behaviour can often appear to be "moral" when viewed from the outside.

Morality is not just a form of instinctive behaviour, like submissive ritual displays that animals use to ensure minimal conflict between rival males. Perhaps one day we will know more precisely what human nature is – how much of it is genetic and how much a result of nurture.

Marx and Economic Determinism

Karl Marx (1818-83) was deeply opposed to the anarchists' benign view of human nature, which he condemned as unscientific and unrevolutionary. Marx declared history to be a series of different ages separated solely by different economic "modes of production" which consequently determined classes and the inevitable struggle between them.

THE DOMINANT CLASS OF ANY ONE HISTORICAL PERIOD WILL CONTROL THE MEANS OF PRODUCTION...

...AND INDIVIDUAL MEMBERS OF THAT CLASS WILL ALWAYS FIGHT FOR THE INTERESTS OF THAT CLASS, OFTEN WITHOUT REALIZING IT!

This is because they are products of that class's **"ideology"**.

An "ideology" is a collection of attitudes, values and beliefs held by groups of people. The "root proposition" of Marx's views on ideology is that "social being determines consciousness". The economic base of society determines its superstructure or its beliefs about everything like family life, religion and ethics.

Capitalism has survived so successfully because the dominant class has monopolized education, religion, the law, the media and philosophy for over 200 years. People may hold different moral views about marriage: that it is a "holy sacrament", a "legal requirement", part of a "system of kinship patterns" and so on. But the "scientific" truth about marriage is its economic basis.

Marx is usually hostile to all moral theorizing and doctrine. So, "morality" is always ideology masking bourgeois or other economic interests.

False Consciousness

An individual may believe he/she is acting on "moral" grounds, but he/she will always be acting in the interests of the predominant class. He/she will be a victim of **"false consciousness"**. This is how ideology functions. It disguises the interest of one class as a universal moral interest.

False consciousness will then be exchanged for **"class consciousness"**: people will not follow a set of moral rules without understanding their economic foundation.

Exactly how the revolutionary proletariat interest is impartially "good" is not very clear. Marx assumes that certain revolutionary intellectuals will remain uncontaminated by false consciousness and so will be sure of their own non-Capitalist moral certainty.

IS THIS NOT **DANGEROUS?**

CAN WE BELIEVE THAT WHEN EVENTUALLY ALL RELIGION, LAW, MORES, PROPERTY AND THE STATE ARE ABOLISHED, SOMEHOW OUR MORAL BELIEFS WILL BE MORE **"OBJECTIVE"?**

Moral Chickens and Class Eggs

Marx's account of morality as a by-product of economic activity also seems odd. Without moral agreements or rules, society itself probably cannot get started, and so would be prior to features like "class" and "means of production". There is, however, clearly a complex and symbiotic relation between economics and morality. If the economic life of any society becomes chaotic, then the moral beliefs of individuals change quite rapidly.

Utilitarianism

Another radically different way of looking "objectively" at morality is
Utilitarianism. Both founders of Utilitarianism were child prodigies.
Jeremy Bentham (1748-1832) could read Latin and Greek when he
was five years old and graduated from Oxford at 16. **J.S. Mill** (1806-
73) could speak fluent Greek at the age of three and was helping his
father to write about economics when he was 14. Both men were
radical empiricists. They thought that knowledge had to come from the
senses and not just be invented by the mind. They were also fiercely
democratic, anti-establishment, anti-monarchist, and anti-imperialist –
rather unwise things to be in late 18th century and Victorian England.

Jeremy Bentham
1748 – 1832

John Stuart Mill
1806 – 1873

Bentham was something of an eccentric recluse, so shy that he couldn't bear to see more than one visitor at a time. He kept rats and a pet pig which followed him around. He also designed a grim totalitarian prison – the Panopticon, so called because its every prisoner could be spied on 24 hours a day. He was a militant atheist and believed that dead relatives shouldn't be buried but stuffed and kept as ornaments in your house.

When he died, his corpse was dissected before a group of friends and relations at University College, London. His skeleton is still there, padded with straw and topped with a wax head.

The Law and Morality

Bentham was a lawyer, and wrote the snappily titled **Introduction to the Principles of Morals and Legislation** in 1789 – the same year as the French Revolution. Bentham thought English law was a mess – largely because it was without any logical or scientific foundation.

Bentham thought that all these explanations were really "nonsense on stilts" or "ipse dixitism" – people saying English law was a good thing simply because they said so.

Bentham decided to make the law and morality "scientific" in the same way that sociology and psychology claim to make the study of human beings "scientific".

Happiness Sums

He began, as moral philosophers often do, with his own definition of human nature. Human beings are "under the governance of two sovereign masters, pain and pleasure". He means that human beings are pleasure-pain organisms who will always seek out pleasure and avoid pain. For Bentham, laws should be passed only if they maximize pleasure and minimize pain for the majority of people.

This is how Utilitarianism works.

INSTEAD OF RELYING ON VAGUE IDEAS ABOUT FEELINGS OR CONSCIENCE, YOU **CLASSIFY** AND **MEASURE** ANY ACTION IN TERMS OF HOW MANY UNITS OF **PAIN** OR **PLEASURE** IT WILL **PRODUCE.**

You then set about doing "happiness sums" with something Bentham called "felicific calculus". (You ask how intense the happiness will be, how long it will last, how likely it is to occur, whether it has any unpleasant side-effects and so on.) You also try to ensure that the happiness is spread as widely as possible, so as to produce what Bentham called "The General Good" or "the greatest happiness of the greatest number".

A Practical Example

Let's say the government wants to pass a law privatizing public utilities, for example. Take water. The public are polled for their opinions and feelings, and sums worked out and legislation passed accordingly.

Pleasure and pain units

+H = This will make me mildly content.

+2H = This will make me quite happy.

+3H = This will make me very happy.

+4H = This will make me ecstatic with joy.

-H = This will slightly displease me.

- 2H = This will make me moderately unhappy.

-3H = This will make me very unhappy indeed.

-4H = This will make me suicidal.

If the opinion poll results are -3.5 million H units of public unhappiness but +5 million H units of happiness, then the water utility gets privatized and is a "good thing". The majority get what they want because Utilitarianism is democratic.

Consequences not Motives

For Utilitarians, motives are unimportant; only consequences count.
The stress is on the act rather than the agent. Bentham and Mill would
argue that people's motives can't be seen or measured, but the
consequences of their actions can be. This is why Utilitarianism is
sometimes also known as "Consequentialism".

In certain rare situations, "Act" Utilitarians are allowed to break
traditional moral rules if by so doing they produce a balance of
happiness over misery. If a Utilitarian brain surgeon and a non-
philosophical beggar were on a waterlogged raft that could only
support one person...

By saving his own life and his medical skills, the murdering surgeon
will bring about more happiness for more people than the beggar will
ever be able to do in the future.

Bentham's disciple John Stuart Mill was force-fed with education until the age of 20 when he suffered a nervous collapse.

He worked as an official in the East India Company, eventually became an MP and led active campaigns for women's suffrage. His most famous books on ethics are **On Liberty** (1858) and **Utilitarianism** (1863).

Mill's Ideas

Mill didn't agree with everything Bentham said. He believed that Utilitarianism could be made into a moral system for ordinary individuals as well as for lawmakers. He was worried about some of Bentham's more vulgar populist attitudes and preferred to talk about "happiness" rather than "pleasure". He thought that Utilitarian morality could be made less materialistic by prioritizing cultural and spiritual kinds of happiness over coarser and more physical pleasures.

IT IS BETTER TO BE A HUMAN BEING DISSATISFIED THAN A PIG SATISFIED...

WHAT ABOUT A DISSATISFIED PIG?

Rule Utilitarians

Mill also thought that most ordinary people should normally stick to traditional moral rules, rather than "calculate" what they should do all the time. Perhaps this makes Mill a "Rule" Utilitarian – someone who believes that morality should still be about obeying moral rules, even if the rules are decided upon Utilitarian grounds. (You only obey those rules which experience has shown will produce the greatest happiness of the greatest number.) Some philosophers believe that morality is a matter of everyone always obeying rules.

Mill's Pluralism

Mill worried about the "tyranny of the majority" in his essay **On Liberty**. He was a great pluralist. A healthy society would be one with a huge variety of different individuals and lifestyles with room for oddballs like New Age Travellers. So long as people don't interfere with the freedoms of others, they should be allowed to think and do what they like.

UTILITARIANS HAVE SOME VERY LIBERAL VIEWS ON THE DECRIMINALIZATION OF "VICTIMLESS CRIMES" LIKE TAKING SOFT DRUGS OR THE PRACTICE OF EUTHANASIA.

BUT, FOR UTILITARIANS, IF THE MAJORITY OF THE POPULATION THINKS IT WOULD BE HAPPY TO SEE NEW AGE TRAVELLERS IN PRISON, THEN THAT'S WHERE WE WILL END UP!

Under a Utilitarian system, the huge amounts of mild happiness registered by the majority will outweigh the much smaller amounts of intense misery that the travellers will feel.

Utilitarianism may not guarantee the rights of individuals or minorities.

What is Happiness?

The philosopher **Bernard Williams** (b. 1929) asks us to imagine a "Hedon machine" that produces instant non-addictive happiness which everyone uses during their leisure time. Most Utilitarians wouldn't find anything wrong with this kind of ersatz happiness, but there seems to be something wrong with the idea of it.

PERHAPS WE THINK THAT PEOPLE ARE MORE THAN JUST PLEASURE-PAIN ORGANISMS...

...PERHAPS WE EVEN **NEED** PAIN NOW AND AGAIN TO MAKE US FULLY HUMAN!

AND IS IT REALLY POSSIBLE TO "MEASURE" AMOUNTS OF SUBJECTIVE HUMAN HAPPINESS AND MISERY LIKE POTATOES IN THE WAY THAT BENTHAM INSISTS YOU CAN?

Happiness for Utilitarians often takes the form of "public good", like libraries, hospitals, schools, good drainage and so on. We may not be able to measure private subjective individual happiness, but perhaps public utilities and the happiness they produce can be measured. Utilitarians at least introduced the radical idea that the chief duty of government is to make the majority of their population happy.

Is It Really Scientific?

A moral philosophy that ignores people's motives seems odd.
We like to think that being moral involves good thoughts as well as
good deeds. And a moral philosophy that lets you break traditional
moral rules "on occasion" is rather disturbing. Would you like to share a
raft with a Utilitarian?
Furthermore, is it true that Utilitarianism can make ethics "scientific"?
Mill tries to do this by a kind of semantic acrobatics – by declaring that
the concept "good" means "the greatest happiness of the greatest
number". But what the majority want isn't always good.

Mill had communitarian ideas about this.

One man who thought he could do that convincingly was Immanuel
Kant.

The Moral Law of Duty

Immanuel Kant (1724-1804) didn't agree with what he'd heard of Utilitarianism, and thought that morality rarely had anything to do with happiness. Kant was born, lived, worked and died in Königsberg, a professional academic paid to study and teach philosophy. He was so ridiculously regular in his habits that people would set their clocks by observing his daily walks through the town.

This he set out to do in **Foundations of the Metaphysics of Morals**.

Practical Reason

Kant started by asking what it is that distinguishes a moral action from a non-moral one. He concluded that a moral action is one which is done from a **sense of duty**, rather than following inclinations or doing what we want. This is why Kant is often known as a **Deontologist**, or believer in duties.

ETHICS IS ALL ABOUT WHAT THESE DUTIES ARE, HOW WE FIND OUT WHAT THEY ARE, AND WHY WE MUST OBEY THEM.

Kant begins with the assertion that humans are rational beings. People have "Theoretical Reason" to enable them to perform complex cerebral tasks like mathematics and logic. They also have "Practical Reason" to service their "good will". "Good will" is the motive that produces our determination to be good people, and our practical reason helps us get there.

Duty versus Inclination

Doing our duty means always obeying certain compulsory moral laws or "imperatives", even if these laws may often seem tiresome or inconvenient to us personally. Being good is hard. It usually involves an internal mental struggle between what our duty is and what we would really like to do. This is where Kant radically differs from the Utilitarians. Deontologists like Kant often appear to be fairly miserable because they always deny themselves pleasures and grimly carry out their moral obligations.

82

The Parable of the Rich Young Man

Kant implies that a naive, rich young man who spontaneously gives money to beggars isn't a moral person. Although the consequences of his instinctive generosity are obviously good for local beggars, he has no idea of what his moral duty is.

He is like a child who accidentally makes the right move in chess. He has no inner understanding of the game's rules or purpose. Morality for Kant is a serious business. It involves choosing **duties**, not wants; **motives** and not consequences are the central distinguishing feature of a moral action. Morality is not about **doing** what comes naturally, but **resisting** what comes naturally.

The Universability Test

Kant explains how we can find out what the compulsory moral rules are. We work them out, not by asking ourselves what we would like to do, but by using our reason. He asks us to imagine what would happen if we "universalized" what we wanted to do, always making sure that we treated people as ends and never as means. Say we wanted to steal. If everyone stole from everybody else all the time then not only would society collapse rather rapidly but, more importantly for Kant, the concept of "stealing" would itself enter a kind of illogical "black hole".

By using our reason and the "Universability Test", we have indirectly discovered a compulsory rule or "**categorical imperative**": Don't steal! This test is like a "moral compass", always revealing the correct "moral north" to us. This test also works against lying. If everybody lied all the time, then truth and meaning would both disappear. So, lying is irrational and not allowed. This is how Kant tries to show us why moral rules are compulsory.

Inflexible Rules

But can we really accept that it is never right to lie?
Kantian ethics sounds too perfect for most human beings. Moral rules
are rather like useful generalizations: in general we think it is best not
to lie, but there are occasionally circumstances where it is obviously
morally correct to do so.

Kant's system of compulsory rules seems monolithic and incredible
because it doesn't allow for exceptions. It also doesn't help us choose
between moral rules. Sometimes it is just not possible to keep a
promise and to tell the truth at the same time.

In this situation it's simply impossible to keep your promise and tell the
truth, and Kant doesn't offer you a method for deciding which rule to
obey.

Moral Imagination

Kant seems to think that as rational beings we "must" be moral, just as we "must" recognize that 2 + 2 "must" be 4. The problem is that the logical necessity of maths is internal to maths itself, whereas ethical choices are not "necessary" like this. Lots of people can and do choose to be wicked and carry out their evil deeds in a rational manner. But Kant is probably right to stress the importance of motive in ethics, and to insist that universality is an essential part of it.

Kant also stresses the importance of **moral imagination**. To be moral, we have always to imagine ourselves as being on the receiving end of other people's decisions. People who are wicked, in other words, may just be unimaginative.

Ethical Doctrines Contrasted

Utilitarians and Deontologists are always arguing about what ethics should be like. Some people think that morality should be pragmatic and take human happiness and personal fulfilment into account. Others think that it should be pure and "above" human desires altogether.

Clearly Utilitarianism offers more flexibility, but Deontologists may protect morality with more vigour and take "backward looking" duties like promise-making more seriously. Both doctrines usually arrive at similar moral destinations, even if their ways of getting there are very different.

Hume's Radical Scepticism

David Hume (1711-76), a Scottish philosopher, asked whether there could be such a thing as moral knowledge. Hume was a radical empiricist and a sceptic. He believed that virtually all knowledge has to come through our senses. Hume invented the type of ethical philosophy often called **meta-ethics** – the study of moral language, its meaning, function and certainty. Meta-ethics doesn't offer anyone moral advice. But its conclusions are often startling.

In his book, **A Treatise of Human Nature** (1740), Hume asks what a statement like "Murder is wrong" actually means.

"Murder is wrong" isn't saying the same sort of thing as "Grass is green", even though it looks grammatically rather similar.

Hume also says that we can't use logic or reason to "prove" the truth of moral beliefs either. The one big rule of deductive logic is that no one is allowed to magic extra information from an argument's premises into a conclusion. If you do this, then your argument isn't valid. Here's an example...

All you can prove from this argument is that Tiddles has fleas, nothing more. Similarly, you can't prove stealing is wrong in a conclusion derived from two factual premises like this...

There's a "gap" here between the factual statements ("is" ones) and moral statements ("ought" ones). The argument is invalid because it "jumps" to conclusions. You can't prove moral beliefs by using logic, which means you can't prove moral propositions just by piling up facts.

So, moral statements are a puzzle because they don't appear to fall into the standard categories of empirical or logical knowledge, which philosophers claim are the only real ones.

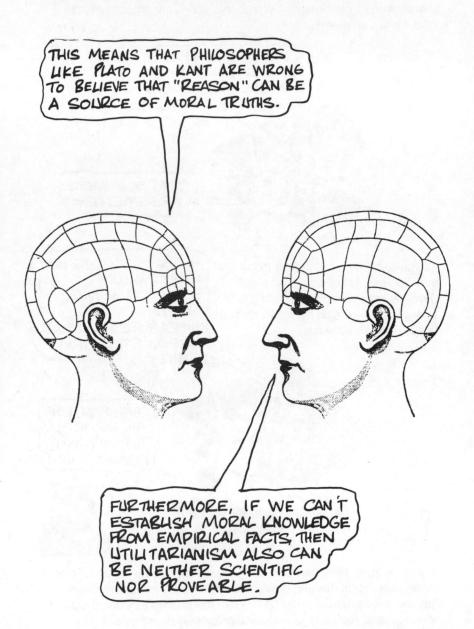

THIS MEANS THAT PHILOSOPHERS LIKE PLATO AND KANT ARE WRONG TO BELIEVE THAT "REASON" CAN BE A SOURCE OF MORAL TRUTHS.

FURTHERMORE, IF WE CAN'T ESTABLISH MORAL KNOWLEDGE FROM EMPIRICAL FACTS, THEN UTILITARIANISM ALSO CAN BE NEITHER SCIENTIFIC NOR PROVEABLE.

Beliefs are Psychological

So what are moral statements? Hume concluded that a statement like "Murder is wrong" is really someone reporting their subjective feelings about murder to us. So, someone who says, "Murder is wrong" merely means "I disapprove of murder".

ALL WE CAN BE CERTAIN OF, FROM SUCH A STATEMENT, IS THE PSYCHOLOGICAL STATE OF MIND OF ONE INDIVIDUAL.

Hume does try to reassure us by emphasizing that we'd all usually have similar feelings to this individual because we are all "sympathetic" beings who instinctively identify with other people in trouble. But the sceptical Hume is determined to show us that there is very little "knowledge" that we can ever be really certain about. Our moral beliefs are **psychological** rather than logical or empirical, but that doesn't mean they are trivial or unimportant. Hume pointed out that there is nothing to stop us organizing society on roughly Utilitarian grounds, to make as many people as happy as we possibly can.

Is the "Is-Ought Gap" True?

Some modern philosophers are now less sure that Hume is right. There is a growing suspicion that the "is-ought gap" may be more of a doctrine than a fundamental truth about ethics. "Facts" like "money" and "debt" exist only against a background of social value judgements. It also doesn't seem true to say that moral words or statements are either wholly factual or wholly moral.

> WORDS LIKE "HOMELESS"...
> ... "FATHER"... "TORTURE"...ALL
> HAVE BOTH A **FACTUAL** AND
> A **MORAL** CONTENT.

We can talk about social and institutional "facts", e.g. promise-keeping, which might produce a valid argument that goes like this...

> I MADE A PROMISE.
> THERE IS AN INSTITUTION OF
> PROMISE-KEEPING IN OUR
> SOCIETY. ———
> THEREFORE I OUGHT TO
> KEEP MY PROMISE.

Subjectivists and Objectivists

Subjectivists agree with Hume that morality is no more than individuals telling us their feelings. They believe that there is no such thing as moral "knowledge" – feelings aren't facts.
Objectivists like Plato and the Utilitarians disagree. Utilitarians are "Naturalists" who believe it possible to make morality a form of empirical and scientific "knowledge". Plato, like most Christians, is a non-naturalist who also believes there is such a thing as moral knowledge, but that it comes to us from a mystical non-empirical source like intuition.

Is moral knowledge possible?
The views of Subjectivists and Objectivists are irreconcilable and odd.

But it also seems odd to claim that there is moral "knowledge". If someone says "There are people living on Jupiter", we know what sort of evidence is needed to prove this statement true or false.

Moral Language is Nonsense

One modern English philosopher, **A.J. Ayer** (1910-89), was as sceptical as Hume about the possibility of ethical "knowledge". Ayer's positivist analysis of moral language is even more aggressive than Hume's. In his **Language, Truth and Logic** (1936), Ayer claimed that moral language is meaningless. A statement like "Murder is wrong" isn't even someone reporting their feelings to us, but just **expressing** them. Ayer's **Emotivism** is sometimes called the "hurrah-boo" theory, because for him someone saying "Murder is wrong" is merely saying "Murder boo!" or making a kind of primitive emotional noise.

THIS MEANS THAT ANY KIND OF ARGUMENT BETWEEN PEOPLE ABOUT A MORAL ISSUE IS UTTERLY FUTILE, UNSOLVEABLE AND IRRATIONAL.

EUTHANASIA, BOO!

HOW ON EARTH COULD WE DECIDE WHO WAS RIGHT IN AN ARGUMENT LIKE THIS?

EUTHANASIA, HURRAH!

In Ayer's view, all "moral philosophy" had been some kind of linguistic and logical error. There is no such thing as moral "knowledge" or certainty, and there can be no moral experts who can tell us what is right or wrong.

Ayer's radical conclusions about the meaninglessness of moral language horrified many British moral "experts". They thought that his logical analysis of ethics would inevitably lead to nihilism and moral chaos.

Prescriptivism

A more recent philosophical analyst, **Richard Hare** (b. 1919), is often known as a **Prescriptivist.** In **The Language of Morals** (1952), Hare claimed that a moral statement like "Murder is wrong" isn't just an expression of feelings, but more like a recommendation or an order, like "Don't murder". In this respect, Hare is Kantian.

I BELIEVE THAT MORALITY IS ABOUT OBEYING ORDERS OR FOLLOWING RULES. MORAL ORDERS ARE UNLIKE ORDINARY ORDERS, HOWEVER, IN THAT THEY ARE **UNIVERSAL** AND NOT **SPECIFIC**.

THIS IS WHY "DON'T STEAL" IS DIFFERENT FROM "DON'T USE A LATHE WITHOUT WEARING GOGGLES."

Hare was convinced that moral language possesses a kind of built-in "logic" of its own because it applies universal rules to specific cases, rather like logic does. So, like Kant, he thought to be wicked was to be inconsistent.

The Importance of the Imagination

Hare also stresses the importance of the imagination in ethics.
If universality is to function as a restraint on our behaviour, we have to
be able to imagine what it would be like to be on the receiving end.

It's also not always clear when Hare would allow you to plead that
you were a "special case". We'd all probably agree that a woman
with a starving child outside a baker's shop could claim exemption
from the "Don't steal" rule, but it's not easy to work out what
"exemption rules" might be like.

Hare's Prescriptivism also has some strange consequences. For
example, it seems odd to say that "Hitler was evil" means "Don't
behave like Hitler" or that "St. Francis was a good man" means "Give
all your property away and preach to the birds". Most people claim
that statements like these are **descriptive** and not prescriptive at all.

Choosing To Be: Existentialism

A more Romantic and individualist philosopher, the Existentialist **Jean-Paul Sartre** (1905-80) believed that every individual is unique and so no one can generalize about "human nature". This means that moral philosophy cannot be derived from a definition of "human nature", whether this be having a purpose (Aristotle), or being rational (Kant), or existing as a pain-pleasure organism (Bentham).

If we are "cowardly" then it is because we have chosen to be "cowardly", not because God or Nature made us that way. Similarly, if we are "wicked", then we can choose not to be so.

Although we are limited in what we can choose by "facticity" (like economics and genetics), according to Sartre we are "totally free" to make ourselves.

Those who deny the fact of this "freedom" are, for Sartre, "inauthentic" cowards and people of "bad faith". Those who seek or give moral guidance or advice are equally foolish and wicked.
Furthermore, as a rule, society constantly restricts our personal freedoms and wants to mould us into "good citizens".

The Student Who Couldn't Decide

In German-occupied France, a student couldn't decide whether to join the Resistance or to stay at home and look after his widowed mother.

There are no moral "systems" or "rules" or "gurus" to help him. He is totally free to choose what to do. He must then be totally responsible for his final decision and all of the "anguish" that may result if he makes the wrong decision. Morality for Sartre centres wholly on the **freedom** of choosing, rather than on what is chosen.

Sartre implies that moral decision-making for the student and for the rest of us is a lonely, intuitive and wholly individual business of making "fundamental choices".

In his essay **Existentialism and Humanism** (1948) he weakens his harsh advice somewhat with Kantian suggestions that good Existentialists will try to live a life of decisions "made as if for all men". But his attempt to drag a moral code out of existential doctrine isn't really convincing. It's his attack on moral belief systems, rules and doctrines that makes the deepest impression.

It also seems odd to believe that Sartre's student has to make any "fundamental" moral choice. Most people would say he is choosing between two rules: Thou shalt protect thy Mum and Thou shalt defend thy country. Sartre's views about our "total freedom" are also strange. Many might claim that their freedom is far from "total".

Sartre's claim for "existential freedom" must be seen against the gloomy wartime background of Nazi-occupied France and the totalitarian nightmare of Fascist regimes spread across Europe and the Far East. What options did the individual have under such conditions but a stark, anguished choice?

No wonder Sartre and the other Existentialists emphasize that the features of individual ethical action are "anguish", "despair", "absurdity" and "courage". Total freedom is paradoxically the only choice which totalitarian **un**-freedom offers. Problems of "human nature", "reason", "utility" and so on, become irrelevant when the stakes are total.

The Road to Postmodernism

The story of post-war ethics is one of accelerated disillusion and uncertainty. There are several reasons for this. One is the change of emphasis in post-war philosophy from the problems of knowledge to the problem of meaning. As we have seen, this brought about the removal of ethics from epistemology.

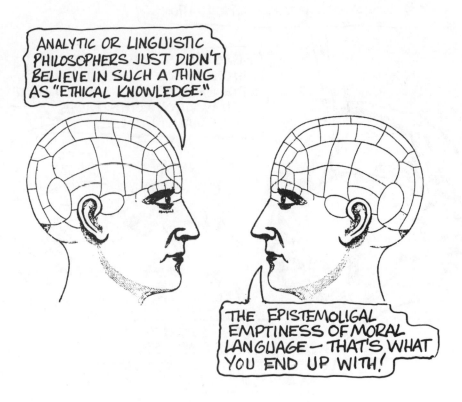

ANALYTIC OR LINGUISTIC PHILOSOPHERS JUST DIDN'T BELIEVE IN SUCH A THING AS "ETHICAL KNOWLEDGE."

THE EPISTEMOLIGAL EMPTINESS OF MORAL LANGUAGE – THAT'S WHAT YOU END UP WITH!

Ethical statements like "stealing is wrong" cannot be verified empirically or guaranteed by logic and so become no more than subjective, emotional utterances. And if all moral philosophy has been doing is to produce "pseudo-propositions" which are nonsensical, then all ethical foundations disappear. We are left with unproveable human beliefs without any foundation and offering no guarantees.

What Is This Thing Called "Human Nature"?

Sartre's point about the "subjectivity" of ethics is an important one, because it re-emphasizes doubts about the traditional definitions of "human nature".

The existence of this huge variety of claims made about human nature probably indicates the difficulties of ever defining it satisfactorily or convincingly. 20th century views about human nature have been shifting rapidly and radically. We can now see more clearly that definitions of human nature are usually ideological artefacts – persuasive myths used by one group to suppress another.

Freud's Model of the Psyche

It is also very difficult to engage in this "definitions exercise" after the introduction of psychoanalysis into the Western intellectual tradition. **Sigmund Freud** (1856-1939) may not be the great scientist he thought he was, but he has radically altered our understanding of ourselves as moral beings.

UNTIL FREUD, MOST MORAL PHILOSOPHERS ASSUMED THAT THE HUMAN MIND IS "OPEN TO INSPECTION."

THEY WORKED ON THE ASSUMPTION THAT WE ARE ALWAYS IN CONTROL OF OUR THOUGHT PROCESSES AND THE CHOICES WE MAKE ARE "**OURS**."

I CHANGED ALL THAT!

Freud's view of human nature is a determinist one. Human beings are programmed by instinctive psychic structures constructed from infancy to maturity in "layers" of the **Unconscious**, **Ego** and **Super-Ego**. The "real" workings of human nature can be viewed most clearly in neurotic and psychotic individuals, or in the dreams or "verbal slips" of "normal" and "healthy" individuals.

The Unconscious and Moral Autonomy

Our Unconscious exerts powerful pressures upon us to fulfil our instinctual desires, which the Super-Ego insists the Ego deny. The Super-Ego is similar to the "conscience"; it is like a parental voice forcefully reminding us of social norms acquired throughout childhood. The conscious Ego spends much of its time refereeing between the authoritative Super-Ego and the equally insistent but more primitive voice of the Unconscious.

This tripartite model of human nature has been criticized as utterly unscientific, which it undoubtedly is. But, as a metaphorical explanation of the human psyche, it has had immense cultural force. Freud stresses the constant and inevitable conflict that must occur between the unconscious desires of the individual and the censoring and controlling forces of civilization.

If we are almost totally ignorant of the real sources of our attitudes, propensities and desires, then how can we ever be fully in control of our moral lives? We may have causes of, and not reasons for, our moral behaviour. If Freud's determinist vision is true, then it places severe limits on any notion of personal moral responsibility.

The necessity of free-will in any moral agent is as old as Aristotle. Hume pointed out that although our actions may be "caused" or "determined" this does not mean that we are "coerced" or "forced" to behave in certain ways.

IF MY ARM JERKS INVOLUNTARILY AND HITS SOMEONE, THEN I AM NOT TO BLAME; BUT IF I **CHOOSE** TO HIT SOMEONE – EVEN IF MY CHOICE IS DETERMINED – THEN I AM RESPONSIBLE FOR WHAT I DID.

BUT I SUGGEST THAT WE DON'T REALLY "OWN" OUR INNERMOST THOUGHTS IN THE WAY THAT HUME BELIEVES WE DO....

Most moral philosophers might say that although Freud may be right to claim that our inner selves can be shaped and governed by both internal and external forces, we are not wholly controlled by them. If we are, then it certainly doesn't feel like that – not many people have a core belief of themselves as moral robots.

Lacan: the Fiction of the "Self"

Freud's most radical modern disciple is **Jacques Lacan** (1901-81).
Lacan is radical because he suggests that the Unconscious is by no
means some primitive entity that we must control through our conscious
selves, but is in fact the "nucleus" of our very being.
"I am where I think not."

According to Lacan, the Unconscious is structured like a language
which is why it often reveals its presence to us through wordplay.
The "self" is therefore essentially linguistic and, since language exists
as a structure before the individual enters into it, then the whole notion
of "human identity" becomes deconstructed and untenable.

The Holocaust and the Betrayal of the Enlightenment

Probably the most important influence on post-war ethics was the Second World War itself. The efficient and "rational" industrialized slaughter of millions of innocent civilians by a civilized Western nation accelerated an erosion of belief in human potential and ethical progress. The horrors of the concentration camps led to a more cynical view of human nature as something nastily Hobbesian, or worse, as something wholly "plastic" and empty, waiting for leaders to do its moral choosing for it.

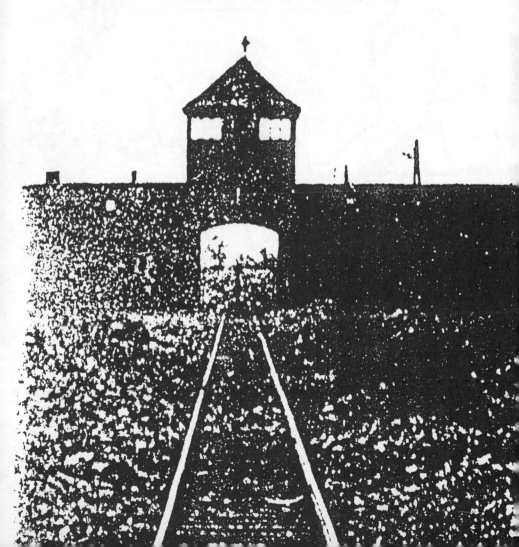

The disturbing combination of the blind obedience of many people to amoral monsters and this systematic pointless extermination of minorities sent many post-war philosophers and thinkers scurrying off to find explanatory theories of all kinds for the mystery of this large-scale evil.

The Dangers of "Reason"

What the war made clear was the role of "reason" in planning and creating so much human suffering. The more intelligent British Enlightenment writers and philosophers, like Hume and Swift, always had deep suspicions about reason as a source of moral wisdom, and constantly undermined it.

More recent "postmodernist" thinkers, such as **Jean-François Lyotard** (b. 1924) and **Jacques Derrida** (b. 1930), are more radical.

Too many philosophers have held an absolute faith in reason and its ability to produce that which is universal, true and eternal. This kind of blindness to the reality (that our beliefs are merely selective and contingent linguistic constructs) can lead to dangerous political certainties which insist on the exclusion of "the other" – sometimes in the form of powerless and vulnerable minorities.

Postmodernist Scepticism

So, ethics is in trouble – its language is merely an expression of emotional noises, the "human nature" on which it is so often based is only a fiction, and our belief in a transcendent "reason" as a source of moral wisdom may produce something very different – efficient evil.

This takes us into the new abyss of **POSTMODERNISM** itself, which has increased ethical scepticism and uncertainty even more. Postmodern philosophers have added to this loss of ethical certainty by a kind of abandoned "celebration of relativism".

It's also more clear now that moral philosophers in the past have been doing little more than playing their own kind of localized language game.

This kind of sceptical conclusion is not new to the 20th century. Protagoras the Sophist said similar things in 5th century B.C. Athens. And much of "postmodern" thinking can be traced back to **Friedrich Nietzsche** (1844-1900) and his blitz on "metaphysics".

Human, All Too Human

Postmodernism has shattered many long-held beliefs. It is wholly sceptical about the existence of some kind of "objective reality" or the possibility of using "reason" to understand it. It is even more doubtful about the existence of any kind of "human nature". This means there is no "Archimedean lever" or supreme principle that can tell us which ethical system is the "best" or the "truest" one. We live in a relativistic universe where there are only human truths and human ethics.

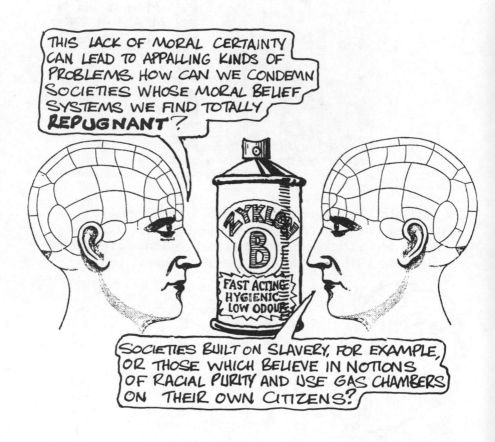

If there are no clear and proveable moral values which we can all agree on and share, then how can we prevent future evils performed by individuals or governments on the rest of us?

Postmodernist Visions: Supermarket Slavery

So what moral futures does Postmodernism offer us? Postmodernism celebrates uncertainty and variety, so it's unlikely to point with certainty to any one ethical destination. But here are a few ...

The late Capitalist future could be one of scarce resources, genetically engineered humans, huge corporate employers of slave labour, and hi-tech surveillance of channel-hopping consumers who inhabit a present-tense world of images. The constant "Spectacle" of consumerist images would control and hypnotize individual citizens to accept the "morality" of Capitalism.

Post-Marxist Critical Theory

These ideas about Capitalist morality and ideology originate from several 20th century thinkers, often loosely and misleadingly categorized as "Marxist". They all tend to emphasize how political our "personal morality" is, and how little of what we believe will genuinely be "ours".

Antonio Gramsci (1891-1937) introduced analytic terms like "hegemony" to help us understand how little freedom we have to think new political or moral ideas.

BECAUSE PEOPLE TEND TO REGARD THEIR SOCIAL WORLD AS "FIXED" OR "EMBEDDED", CAPITALIST CLASSES AND GOVERNMENTS ARE ABLE TO CONTROL POPULATIONS BY PERSUADING THEM THAT A CAPITALIST SOCIETY IS "NATURAL" AND "COMMON-SENSICAL".

Gramsci stressed the crucial role of the ideological superstructure (schools, churches, the media, families etc.) in manufacturing the consent of ordinary people in their own oppression.

Herbert Marcuse (1898-1979) subsequently explained how Capitalism forces people to see themselves primarily as "one dimensional" isolated consumers with false needs.

I SHOP, THEREFORE I AM.

Capitalist States produce "closed" forms of discourse, so that alternative views are made virtually impossible.

HUMAN SOCIETIES SECRETE IDEOLOGY AS THE VERY ELEMENT AND ATMOSPHERE INDISPENSIBLE TO THEIR HISTORICAL RESPIRATION AND LIFE.

Roland Barthes (1915-80) emphasized the point that "reality" is made; it is a social construct that derives meaning from a complex system of signs. So, whoever has the dominant discourse can determine what is "real".

Michel Foucault (1926-84) extended Marx's views about knowledge as a form of "ideological construct". For Foucault, knowledge is a "construct" used by the powerful to oppress the weak.

MUCH OF WHAT IS CULTURAL AND POLITICAL IS "NATURALIZED" INTO WHAT IS "COMMON SENSE" ...IT "GOES WITHOUT SAYING."..

BY CLAIMING THE TERRITORIES OF "REASON" AND WHAT IS PERMISSABLE AS THOUGHT AND BEHAVIOUR, THE POWERFUL ARE ABLE TO CONVINCE EVERYONE THAT WHAT IS "LOCAL" AND "REGIONAL" IS IN FACT UNIVERSAL AND SO **UNQUESTIONABLE.**

Barthes uses the term "myths" to describe ideological constructs that parade as being "natural". An obvious example would be the myths or ideological constructs about "the poor".

THOSE WHO DISSENT ARE THEN CATEGORIZED AS MAD OR IRRATIONAL AND CAN BE DEALT WITH ACCORDINGLY.

THE POOR ARE WORKSHY, PROBLEMATIC FOR THE REST OF US, THEY CAN'T BUDGET, THEY HAVE LOW INTELLIGENCE AND ARE "ALWAYS WITH US".

117

Nietzschean Dandyism

There are alternative postmodernist visions of our ethical future which are less bleak. **Richard Rorty** (b. 1931), the American pragmatist philosopher, suggests that everyone accept and celebrate the postmodernist vision in which any notions of "knowledge" and "objectivity" have vanished. Thinkers and writers must become Romantics who invent their own private "ethics of taste". Postmodern intellectuals should now adopt a playful distrust of large-scale moral truths and Utopian visions, and cultivate an ironically detached attitude towards all human beliefs, including their own.

WE CAN THEREFORE PURSUE A LIFE OF CURIOSITY WHICH WILL BE COMIC, PLAYFUL, FREE AND INVENTIVE.

IT'S AN EXISTENTIAL OR NIETZSCHEAN VISION IN WHICH THE INDIVIDUAL IS ON A CONTINUAL QUEST FOR "SELF-ENRICHMENT" AND "SELF-ENLARGEMENT" IN A WORLD OF RELATIVE VALUES.

So Rorty's morality is a private one, not much concerned with group welfare – which probably leads to a kind of political quietism. But if there are to be no more ethical "grand narratives", as Lyotard claims, perhaps playful deconstruction and irony are all that is left? Perhaps.

The Evils of Modernism

In **Intimations of Postmodernity**, the sociologist **Zygmunt Bauman** (b. 1925) has attempted to make a series of predictions about what a future postmodernist society might be like. Like Lyotard and **T.W. Adorno** (1903-69), Bauman is deeply hostile to the political agendas of **Modernism** and its dream of total order imposed by governments with their naive faith in "progress" and "reason". Modernism has been a "long march to prison", producing this century's "panopticon societies". Totalitarian States (Modernism's most devout disciples), are now revealed to us as ecologically disastrous and morally repugnant.

MY POINT IS THAT IT WAS PRECISELY BECAUSE THESE SOCIETIES HAD A FIRMLY HELD BELIEF IN THE **OBJECTIVITY** OF THEIR UTOPIAN VISIONS THAT THEY WERE SO APPALLINGLY ABSOLUTIST AND COERCIVE.

Moral Philosophers and Legislators

Philosophers and other legislative intellectuals must take some of the blame for the disasters of Modernism. Plato's confident dream of "philosopher kings" with absolute power has been a seductive one. Many moral philosophers, like Kant, believed in the absolute objectivity of "reason" as the source of their legislative authority. This belief in ethical certainty has been infectious – it helped to reinforce the unassailable confidence of governments in their knowledge as to what was best for those they controlled. Postmodernist philosophers no longer have faith in "foundational philosophies" of this kind, and stress the need for a plurality of moral and political beliefs and interpretations.

Postmodernist Societies

So, we are all now living in a postmodern society. There is no going back. And, as Lyotard has suggested, our postmodern world will become increasingly "atomized" now that the political and intellectual "grand narratives" have lost their credibility. Capitalism and consumerism will probably thrive – a postmodernist society demands variety, something Capitalism is good at providing.

Because there can no longer be any grand political or moral narratives, ethical debates may centre increasingly on single-issue campaigns in a "no man's land of indifference and apathy", says Bauman.

The Postmodernist Moral Agent

The most important feature of postmodernist ethics, as far as the individual is concerned, is the lack of any universally shared moral values. The philosophers were wrong – there are no objective "translocal" moral truths. This means that there will be more ethical confusion and uncertainty. Moral choices will have to made without the reassurance of philosophical foundations.

The postmodern human condition is, more than anything else, a "state of mind". Anyone who has to make moral choices will find no reliable signposts pointing out the road to righteousness. We will have to rely on constant self-monitoring, self-evaluation and a frequent "sharpening up" of our moral awareness. This means that there will be a healthy emphasis on moral debate and ethical difference, and new questions about our rights and skills as moral agents. There will be risk-taking and uncertainty about moral issues.

A Postmodern Hope: Neo-Tribes

Postmodernism means "the exhilarating freedom to pursue anything and the mind-boggling uncertainty as to what is worth pursuing and in the name of what one should pursue it".

According to Bauman, this kind of personal moral freedom could lead in many directions. It could lead to an open, tolerant society of pragmatic individuals continually engaged in ethical debate. Bauman's fear and loathing of 20th century modernist collectivist Utopias means that he is more positive than some about the opportunities that may be offered to us in a postmodern world.

"Neo-tribes", unlike traditional tribes (whose authority is based on coercion and hereditary power), would consist of voluntary members who share certain values and "language-games" and have a tribal identity based on "self-identification". This vision of a series of small-scale societies has its dangers, though. Small communities with shared sets of moral values tend to exclude, as well as include, and may well become competitive and intolerant.

THIS MEANS THAT THE NECESSITY OF TOLERANCE MUST BE CONSTANTLY STRESSED.

A TOLERANCE THAT CELEBRATES AND VALUES DIFFERENCE AND REFUTES ANY "MONOLOGISTIC" CERTAINTIES.

But whatever the future, we postmoderns should all now be more aware how slippery, undesirable and fictional are all the paths to any ethical rainbowland.

Social Ethics

The humbler aims of moral philosophy in a postmodernist age may concentrate on more modest suggestions.

Two philosophers who take this kind of approach are John Rawls and Alasdair MacIntyre.

John Rawls (b. 1921) is a philosopher less interested in grand moral "narratives" and more in what social and legal agreements are necessary to produce a just society. (These "minimum requirements" which ensure a balance between the needs of the individual and society have also been explored by others in "game theory".) If Rawls' philosophy were adopted, then it might help a rather grim-looking late Capitalist future become more humane.

The Future Community: a New Social Contract

Rawls' **A Theory of Justice** attempts to derive ethics from a new kind of social contract. Rawls asks us to imagine a group of rather odd ahistorical beings who come together to agree on a future community in which they and their children will live.

The "veil of ignorance" ensures that the least privileged members of this society will get some protection, because everyone will want to insure themselves against a possible future life of poverty. Rawls suggests that such a group would emerge with the two principles of "liberty" and "difference". Everyone would want to be free to lead their own lives and yet have different goals in life.

Social Justice

In a few years' time, some dynamic and entrepreneurial individuals would be better off than others.

If, however, the majority are offered what is sometimes called "trickle down", then they might feel that the deal is a bad one. Certainly, many people living in Western-style Capitalist economies, seeing their standard of living and job security being rapidly eroded, might welcome a Rawlsian society.

Bring Back Aristotle

For several years now, the philosopher **Alasdair MacIntyre** (b. 1929) has been suggesting that ethics should concentrate less on individuals and their private moral decisions and more on the community and its moral health and welfare. New Aristotelians, like MacIntyre, suggest that ethics should be concentrating more on the people we should be, rather than the things we do. This kind of moral philosophy is usually known as "Virtue Theory".

MacIntyre thinks that modern ethics is in deep trouble. He is critical of much modern ethical philosophy because it just covers the internecine warfare between Deontologists and Utilitarians, or it is unsympathetically analytic and theoretical. MacIntyre's approach to ethics is historical.

I BEGIN BY EXAMINING THE BELIEFS OF THE ATHENIANS IN THE "VIRTUES" THAT THEY THOUGHT WERE NECESSARY FOR ANYONE WHO WISHED TO BE A "SUCCESSFUL" HUMAN BEING.

THE VIRTUES WE ORIGINALLY REGARDED AS ESSENTIAL WERE THOSE VITAL TO THE SURVIVAL OF SMALL, THREATENED COMMUNITIES: STRENGTH, COURAGE AND COMRADESHIP.

WHEN GREEK SOCIETY BECAME MORE SOPHISTICATED, OTHER VIRTUES LIKE JUSTICE, (LEGAL AND DISTRIBUTIVE), TEMPERANCE AND WISDOM GOT ADDED.

SO FOR US ATHENIANS, WORDS LIKE "A GOOD MAN" HAD A VERY CONCRETE, FACTUAL MEANING.

Why Has Ethics Become a Mess?

According to MacIntyre, this kind of Greek moral certainty has been eroded by sceptics like Hume and Ayer. Kant made morality a cold and unsympathetic exercise in reason, and the Utilitarians reduced it to a set of pseudo-scientific calculations that don't work. All such doctrines, whether "Enlightenment" or "Victorian", are also wrong to think that their particular ethics are "objective", when they are peculiarly "local".

We live, according to MacIntyre, in a world of "bureaucrats, aesthetes" and "therapists".

Hope in Traditions

It's a pessimistic view of ethical and philosophical history. MacIntyre does stress, though, that there is still hope. Human beings are unstoppably communitarian – at work, in sports, in charity work and in all forms of human activities. Communal life is held together by traditions and by those dispositions or virtues that groups encourage in individual members.

He suggests that what we need is a new kind of ethical philosophy. One of Aristotle's central ideas is that we should habituate people into having good dispositions towards others, so that moral behaviour becomes almost instinctive, rather than depending on moral "systems". MacIntyre is a bit vague about what these dispositions or virtues are that would produce "moral behaviour", although he does suggest that the "wisdom of the ages" would tell us.

The State We're In

There is certainly a growing belief amongst many moral philosophers and political commentators that MacIntyre and Aristotle may be on to something important here. If, as the millennium approaches, we believe that both society and personal morality are breaking down, then perhaps philosophers should examine more deeply the connections between the two. **Will Hutton**'s recent book on "the State of the Nation" is clearly enthusiastic about this kind of communitarianism:

"What is needed is the development of a new conception of citizenship. Britain must…equip itself with a constitution that permits a new form of economic, social and political citizenship. Economic citizenship will open the way to the reform of financial and corporate structures; social citizenship will give us the chance of constructing an intelligent welfare state based on active solidarity; and political citizenship opens the way to political pluralism and genuine cooperation."

The State We're In, Will Hutton, 1995

What Are the Virtues?

There is at least one major problem which the new Aristotelians have to solve. What will the virtues be? Do virtues exist that we can derive from the "wisdom of the ages" and consequently encourage?
Other postmodernist philosophers would be very doubtful of such a "search". Different cultures would undoubtedly insist on different "virtues" that they felt were appropriate for their members.

And Where is Postmodernism Going?

It's still too early to say with any confidence what postmodernist ethics will be. It may not exist as something we would normally recognize as "ethics" at all. At the moment it looks as if it may be a rather odd combination of the sort of corrosive scepticism of the Ancient Greek Cynics and the healthy pragmatism of Aristotle. It seems wise in its insistence that there are no grand moral truths. Postmodernists seem sensible to stress that we should be wary of philosophers and politicians who claim both that such truths exist and that they personally have some kind of access to them.

Aristotle always maintained that ethics was just a branch of politics and not metaphysics, and writers as diverse as Rawls, MacIntyre and Bauman seem to agree.

Time for a New Feminist Ethics

Some feminist philosophers, like **Martha Nussbaum** (b. 1947), believe that it is men who like to invent elaborate abstract formal "systems" which they then try to impose on the messier world of human beings and their moral problems.

Mary Wollstonecraft (1759-97) attacked this view of female "nature" as an ideological construct whose primary function is to legitimize male supremacy in public life.

> THERE IS AN OBVIOUS DIFFERENCE BETWEEN THE BIOLOGICAL "SEX" OF WOMEN. AND THEIR SOCIALLY AND CULTURALLY DETERMINED "GENDER."

> SO THE DOCTRINE OF AN ESSENTIALIST "FEMALE NATURE" IS A PROBLEM FOR ANY FEMINIST ETHIC, IF "FEMALE NATURE" IS REALLY A SOCIAL AND HISTORICAL CONSTRUCT.

Julia Kristeva (b. 1941) stresses that there is no such thing as "essential woman", primarily because of postmodernist doubts about the very notion of "identity" itself.

135

Private and Public Spheres

But some feminists believe there may be something attractive about these traditional gender "virtues" entering the sphere of public life.

They argue that some of the traditional "female virtues" of cooperation and caring that operate in the "private sphere" should be given a much higher priority in the brutal and ruthless masculine "public sphere".

Sensible Jake and Sensitive Amy

One good example of the different "feminist" approach to moral dilemmas was exhibited by "Amy" in **Lawrence Kohlberg**'s famous study of moral development, the **Philosophy of Moral Development**, 1981.

Two children, "Jake" and "Amy", were presented with a moral dilemma.

SHOULD A POOR MAN STEAL FROM A CHEMIST'S SHOP THE DRUGS NEEDED BY HIS DYING WIFE?

What did sophisticated Jake (an act Utilitarian), say?

Amy, surprisingly, had another answer.

YES!

THE HUSBAND SHOULD GO AND EXPLAIN HIS POSITION TO THE CHEMIST —

— AND SEE IF A SOLUTION CAN BE FOUND THAT WAY.

So, perhaps Jake is wrong to believe that moral problems can be "solved" by one solitary individual aggressively applying a moral "system". The inference is that women look at specifics of the relationships and emotions involved in moral dilemmas, and then try to negotiate.

But it's still not that clear that there are predictable differences in the ways that men and women approach moral issues. To suggest that women are less rational and more "intuitive" could easily be depicted as a weakness rather than a strength. Many philosophers believe that one central feature of ethics is its universality, and would worry about the notion of "negotiation" in moral dilemmas. (Suppose "Amy" isn't very good at persuasive negotiation, for instance?)

Different Moral Priorities

Perhaps a better way of looking at this difference is not to claim that women think about moral issues in different ways, but to show how their moral priorities are different.

But child-rearing practices are as much cultural as "biological", and it is difficult to see how they could be used as a basis for a radical new set of universal, gender-neutral ethical "virtues" that could be encouraged in everyone.

S.H.E.

It is a truth universally unacknowledged that moral doctrines and systems have all emerged from societies which place women in a subordinate position. If those concerns and activities that have been traditionally associated with women were given a superior status to those traditionally associated with men, then moral priorities might become very different.

The answer might well be a **S.H.E.** (Sane, Humane, Ecological) society.

Environmental Ethics

One moral question really unique to our own century is that of our relationship to the natural environment. This question has arisen partly as a result of the startling human population explosion of recent years and the alarming growth of new industrialized societies, first in the West and now in the Far East. Both have produced pollution of the planet on an unprecedented scale.

We need to agree about our behaviour towards our planet, even more than we need detailed scientific information about the damage we are doing. We have to find alternative economic, political and cultural ideologies which are very unlike those we currently support.

Anthropocentric Ethics

At present no one is wholly sure what "environmental ethics" means or looks like. Traditional ethical doctrines have always been selfishly anthropocentric.

I WAS ONLY EVER INTERESTED IN HUMAN POTENTIAL AND HAPPINESS.

OUR DUTIES ARE EXCLUSIVELY TOWARDS OTHER MEMBERS OF OUR OWN SPECIES.

UTILITARIANS HAVE ALWAYS PRIORITIZED HUMAN HAPPINESS.

WHAT WE NEED IS SOME KIND OF ETHIC WHICH IS LESS SELFISHLY HUMAN AND MORE "HOLISTIC."

It would have to be able to arbitrate between a complex series of empirical planetary facts and human ideologies and values. There is not much moral philosophy we can plunder from the past to help us.

PERHAPS BUDDHISM'S EMPHASIS ON SIMPLICITY AND FRUGALITY AS INTRINSIC VALUES MAY BE A USEFUL START.

The Newbury Case

Few people now believe that material wealth and jobs must be pursued relentlessly, whatever the environmental cost. Governments may be more ethically challenged than ordinary people in this respect. The current British government is still heavily committed to the "car culture" although it is at last beginning to recognize the damage that cars and lorries do to the countryside and to the lives of citizens in urban environments.

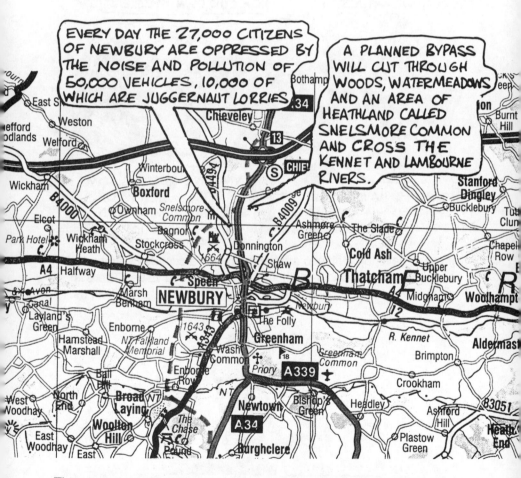

The common and the rivers are "Sites of Special Scientific Interest". The new road will probably destroy or severely damage a rare local colony of nightjars and there is even a slight chance that, by diverting one of the rivers, a rare species of river snail will become extinct.

Does it Matter?

A Utilitarian Argument

One common ethical and environmental argument is the human-centred Utilitarian one.

This familiar Utilitarian kind of argument is powerful but still places only human happiness at its centre. Nightjars and trees have moral value only insofar as they give human beings **pleasure**.

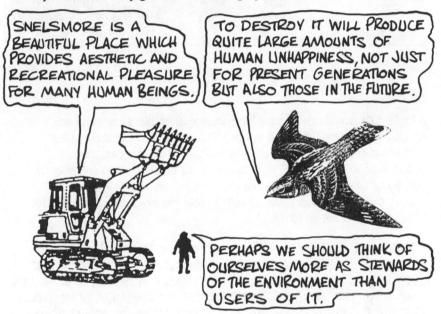

Another kind of ethical-environmental argument allows for the moral rights of nightjars and badgers to pursue their own "interests", which they can no longer do if their habitat is utterly destroyed. This might be called the "enlightened Utilitarian" argument, which recognizes the intrinsic value of the sentient and conscious lives of species other than ourselves. This argument would stress how the animals' habitat is a **need**, whereas our human motorway is only a **want**.

But what about non-sentient entities like trees or rocks? An extremely enlightened and rather unorthodox Utilitarian might claim that trees also have "interests" – they need an environment in which to flourish and be healthy and this would be destroyed or damaged by any pollution of the immediate environment.

Holistic Ethics

A Utilitarian would have no problem in admitting plants or even soil, rocks and water to the moral sphere, but really only because of the sentient life forms they support. A holistic ethic would grant moral importance to non-sentient entities like rocks and trees on very different grounds, by citing their intrinsic values of "diversity", "interrelatedness" and "ecological richness", all values independent of their usefulness to us or other sentient life forms.

To produce such a planet might be thought of as wicked as well as unimaginative. Perhaps, to be fully human, we need areas of wilderness so that we can occasionally escape from a wholly manufactured environment where all we ever see is other humans.

We Are Not Outsiders

This failure of traditional Utilitarian arguments to produce moral answers suggests to some that we need a newer, more complex kind of ecological ethic which is more radically "holistic". It is going to be difficult for us to grasp this new kind of ethic, because it does require a considerable effort of the imagination, and a readiness on our part to reject our own immediate material desires in favour of something remoter and grander. Traditional ethics doesn't account for this, as an inevitably human-centred activity. As far as we know, nightjars and trees don't go in for it.

BUT THIS DOESN'T MEAN THAT HUMAN BEINGS MUST ALWAYS RELENTLESSLY TAKE MORAL PRECEDENCE OVER ALL OTHER LIFE FORMS FOR EVER AND EVER.

FOR A LONG TIME, WE HUMANS HAVE BEHAVED AS IF SOMEHOW WE ARE "OUTSIDE" OF OUR ECOLOGICAL ENVIRONMENT... ...A BELIEF OFTEN ENCOURAGED BY PHILOSOPHERS.

BUT WE'RE NOT "OUTSIDE". WE NEED AN ETHIC WHICH ENABLES OR EVEN FORCES US TO IDENTIFY WITH THE WHOLE OF THE NATURAL WORLD, OF WHICH WE ARE JUST A PART.

We are members of a complex biosphere whose stability, health and integrity it is in our interest to preserve and not to threaten.
An environmental ethic will have to stress how we must see ourselves as products and perhaps partners of this planet, and not controllers and exploiters of it.

James Lovelock's now famous "Gaia" hypothesis states that our host planet is itself a huge, ruthlessly self-regulating biological organism. This means that it is not committed to the preservation of human life at all. So, it may be very much in our own interest to convince our planetary host that we are worth keeping on as environmentally conscientious house-guests.

ETHICS AND ANIMALS

The Libellous Philosophers

Animals, on Snelsmore Common and elsewhere, are mobile sentient organisms – a class that includes everything from amoebae to chimpanzees. We eat them, use them as unpaid workers, as transport, as entertainment and as experimental tools. Most philosophers have done them no favours. Aristotle thought that animals often mimic what human beings do …

BUT THEY'RE NOT REALLY "DOING" THESE THINGS BECAUSE THERE'S NO THOUGHT "BEHIND" WHAT THEY'RE DOING.

Descartes maintained that animals were machines that could neither think nor feel pain …

Kant thought that it was wrong to be cruel to animals.

AN ANIMAL SCREAMING IN PAIN IS LIKE A CHIMING CLOCK.

SOLELY BECAUSE THIS CRUELTY MIGHT BRUTALIZE INDIVIDUALS AND CONSEQUENTLY MAKE THEM CRUEL TO HUMANS TOO.

Wittgenstein maintained that thinking is impossible without any kind of language.

SO ANIMALS CANNOT BE "CONSCIOUS".

Animal Rights

Many animal activists think that animals have moral or natural "rights" that must be respected. "Rights talk" is usually used by the weak to defend themselves against the powerful. The "weak" can be ordinary citizens fighting against authoritarian governments, minorities attempting to defend themselves against hostile majorities or, in this case, the defenders of animals who wish to stop animals from being mistreated. Moral or legal rights are usually backed up by the underlying doctrine of contracts. Citizens will agree to obey reasonable government laws, if the government does not become tyrannical.

BOTH SIDES THEREFORE GAIN BENEFICIAL RIGHTS AND OBLIGATORY DUTIES.

BUT ANIMALS CAN'T MAKE CONTRACTS!

BECAUSE AN ELEPHANT CAN'T MAKE CLEAR VERBALLY WHAT ITS INTERESTS ARE, THEN IT HAS NO RIGHTS.

"RIGHTS TALK" DOESN'T SEEM TO HELP ANIMALS MUCH EITHER.

147

Can We Prove That Animals Have Rights?

There have been attempts to circumvent this problem of "rights and contracts". You can say that human defenders of animals make contracts on their behalf – just as adults do for inarticulate, immature infants. You can claim that animals have innate rights, but this is rather hard to prove. You can claim that such rights are intuitively self-evident to any rational being – a claim that might well be countered by any battery chicken farmer. More convincingly, you can make the teleological claim that animals have certain kinds of functions to which they have rights.

This argument claims that functions and rights have the same meaning, but they don't really. A man can have the correctly designed organs necessary to fertilize other female human beings, but this doesn't give him the right to do so.

The Utilitarian Argument

On the whole, it seems best to abandon all moral or natural "rights talk". Legal rights are much easier to defend, simply because we know exactly what we are referring to. Either it is illegal to tear badgers to pieces with dogs or it isn't, in which case the badger has certain minimal rights. Whether badgers actually do have enough protection in law is another matter.

Another philosophical way of defending animals is the Utilitarian argument. As we now know, Utilitarians are in favour of producing the greatest happiness for the greatest number.

Getting its needs, wants and interests satisfied probably makes an animal happy in its own way.

Animals and Pain

We can't prove that animals experience pain, but then we can't prove that other human beings apart from ourselves do either. Nevertheless, we would be surprised if they didn't.

The major Utilitarian breakthrough was to change the way of looking at the animals issue. Rationalist philosophers argued about the reasoning and linguistic abilities of animals in an attempt to show whether they had rights or not. Bentham said: "The question is not, Can they reason? nor Can they talk? but, Can they suffer?".

Animals are not things. Morally, they count because they are sentient. Human beings have the nasty habit of denying justice to those unimaginatively perceived of as "outsiders". For the Athenians, anyone who was not Athenian was of no moral importance. Then reluctantly some Athenians included all those who spoke Greek.

But not many Utilitarians think that animals have exactly the same moral status as human beings. They usually maintain that human life and happiness is more complex and so usually takes precedence over animal happiness.

Animal Experiments

A Utilitarian is obliged to recognize the reality and nastiness of animal suffering when deciding the "right" and "wrong" of animal experiments. Every year, millions of animals throughout the world are blinded, burnt, paralyzed, electrocuted, given cancer, brain-damaged and then killed.

Behaviour normally regarded as loathsome is accepted if it is performed by people in white coats with a specific scientific agenda. Some scientists will maintain that it is always permissible for human beings to protect themselves at the expense of the suffering of other species – even if the danger stems from a new brand of cosmetic!

Some animal activists will claim that animals are our moral equals and that to experiment on powerless four-legged conscripts is always wrong. They will point out that animals are often a poor substitute for humans – but at the same time paradoxically stress how closely matched is the DNA between us and many primates.

The Conscientious Scientist and Some Possible Moral Guidelines

A Utilitarian scientist who had the interests of humans and animals at heart might say something like this …

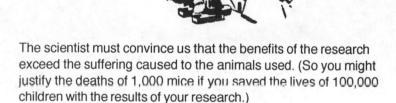

Experiments on animals can be justified on medical grounds only. Any scientist who wishes to experiment on animals must say clearly what medical benefits his research will produce. The scientist must prove to us that his research could not have been performed in any other way (such as by a use of human cell cultures, demographic surveys, computer modelling and so on).

The scientist must convince us that the benefits of the research exceed the suffering caused to the animals used. (So you might justify the deaths of 1,000 mice if you saved the lives of 100,000 children with the results of your research.)

The scientist must declare openly that he would be prepared to conduct the same experiments on brain-damaged infants. (This tests that he is very convinced of the seriousness of what he is doing, and that he is not "species-ist" – treating animals as things.)

Some scientists would object that such stringent rules might stop all "pure" research. Others would say that the price animals have to pay to satisfy human curiosity is too high.

The Persons Argument

The "persons argument" is different. The word "person" is employed by philosophers to avoid the ambiguity and confusion caused by words like "human being" in moral argument. When someone says that a coma patient who has been unconscious for three years is no longer a "human being", they don't mean that the patient has gradually changed into a giraffe, but that they are no longer a "person" or someone with a biography.

Although we would probably consider someone who had lost their memory and refused to speak still to be a person, someone who had none of these attributes we would probably consider not to be. (Perhaps because they were in a terminal coma.)

Are Chimpanzees Persons?

Using such criteria, we would consider the fictional E.T. a "person" even though E.T. clearly isn't human. More importantly, many people would include some higher mammals – great apes, whales, dolphins and others. There is some good evidence to show that some great apes are self-aware, rational, planners, and even language-users in a very limited sort of way.

THIS MEANS THAT CHIMPANZEES AND GORILLAS ARE **PERSONS**--

-- AND TO USE THEM IN EXPERIMENTS IS EQUIVALENT TO USING HUMAN BEINGS WITH SIMILAR LEVELS OF ABILITY.... 4-YEAR-OLD **CHILDREN**, SAY!

If we emphasize the fact that as humans we are different from animals only in degree and not in kind, then perhaps there might be a different set of attitudes to our relationship with them. There is now a strong campaign to give the great apes full human rights for these reasons.

ETHICS AND EUTHANASIA

The Case of Dr Cox and Mrs Boyes

In 1992, Dr Nigel Cox was sent to trial for ending the life of Mrs Lillian Boyes. Mrs Boyes had been one of his patients and a good friend for thirteen years.

SHE SUFFERED FROM INTENSE ARTHRITIC PAIN. FIVE DAYS BEFORE SHE DIED, MRS. BOYES ASKED ME TO STOP HER SUFFERING BY ENDING HER LIFE.

Dr Cox tried to do this by giving her a large dose of heroin, but this seemed to make the pain she experienced worse. Finally he gave her an injection of potassium chloride which may well have finally killed her. Both her sons agreed with what Dr Cox had done, and believed he had "looked after our mother with care and compassion".

The Trial

Dr Cox was arrested and tried for murder. At the end of his trial, Mr Justice Ognall told him …

WHAT YOU HAVE DONE IS NOT ONLY CRIMINAL, IT WAS A TOTAL BETRAYAL OF YOUR UNEQUIVOCAL DUTY AS A **PHYSICIAN**.

Dr Cox got a suspended sentence of twelve months. He was not, however, struck off the medical register by the General Medical Council, and continues to practise medicine. He still thinks he did the right thing for Mrs Boyes.

IT WAS A BONA FIDE ACT THAT WAS SOLELY IN THE INTERESTS OF MRS. BOYES. IT SEEMS SOMEWHAT HARSH TO CRIMINALIZE ME FOR DOING MY BEST IN WHAT WERE QUITE EXCEPTIONAL CIRCUMSTANCES.

Dr Cox clearly did something that was illegal, but was what he did morally wrong?

Is Euthanasia Acceptable?

This now famous legal case illustrates some of the main features of the ethical dilemma of euthanasia – "bringing about a gentle and easy death, especially in the case of an incurable and painful disease." Suicide is no longer illegal in Britain, but euthanasia is, primarily because it involves more than one person – usually close relatives and/or members of the medical profession. There is a wide range of opinion on the subject.

Most people respect life, yet at the same time want to help any human being who is in severe pain. There are no easy answers.

Euthanasia is a major moral dilemma for doctors, patients and many others involved. Few people seriously think that all permanent coma patients have to be kept alive on machinery for ever (although some do), and few people believe that a patient has to endure appalling untreatable pain for as long as possible (although some do). Some doctors and philosophers would say that their job is to save and preserve life and not to take it.

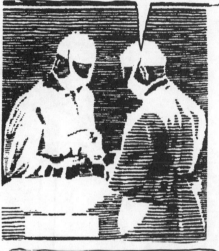

Arguments Against Euthanasia

The arguments against euthanasia are quite powerful. Most people believe that there is something intrinsically wicked about killing people. Some claim that life is "sacred" and only God or Nature has the right to take it away. The "slippery slope" argument reinforces this view.

Once human life is regarded as disposable or cheap, then civilized moral values are in great danger.

Counter Arguments

Others argue that euthanasia is the "easy way out". It may discourage research into pain relief, cures for cancer and so on. Some argue that doctors and nurses may become brutalized or psychologically damaged if they are asked to kill, and that consequently other patients may fear them.

The Coma Patient

In cases of **non-voluntary** euthanasia, the onus is on doctors, relatives and others to decide on behalf of the unconscious, or the just born – all those who are unable to choose.

Philosophers in these instances will sometimes try to distinguish between someone "having a life" and "being alive" – the difference between biography and biology. Other philosophers like to talk about "persons".

You can try to decide what to do by employing Utilitarian pain and pleasure "sums". However, for coma patients who have little chance of recovery, the standard Utilitarian considerations of pain and pleasure seem irrelevant.

SO YOU'D HAVE TO EVALUATE, NOT THE VICTIM'S FUTURE PAIN OR PLEASURE, BUT ASK INSTEAD WHETHER THEY WERE STILL "PERSONS" CAPABLE OF "WORTHWHILE LIVES."

HERE, THERE ARE CLEARLY MAJOR PROBLEMS: HOW CAN YOU DEFINE SUCH VAGUE CRITERIA AS "PERSONS" AND "WORTHWHILE LIVES" — — AND WHO HAS THE **RIGHT TO DECIDE?**

Let Nature Take Its Course

The Acts and Omissions doctrine often applies in these situations.

The Acts and Omissions guideline is a legal rather than moral distinction. It is hardly more moral to ignore a drowning man than actively to drown him. It may often be equally unclear whether the immoral act would be actively to kill someone in severe pain, rather than letting them die slowly by withdrawing treatment. Doing the latter would at least keep the doctor out of the courts.

Let The Patient Decide

Voluntary euthanasia is when the patient is fully conscious and able to request his or her own death.

What Do The Philosophers Say?

Kant

Kant and his followers offer conflicting advice here. A Kantian doctor who frowned on the moral laxity of someone who opted for suicide might find it hard to deny a patient's freely chosen right to decide his/her own fate: Kant places a high value on autonomy. He thought suicide was wrong, although his arguments against it aren't very convincing.

> PERMITTING EUTHANASIA UNIVERSALLY WOULD DESTROY OUR UNDERSTANDING OF THE INTRINSIC VALUE OF HUMAN LIFE.

But several modern philosophers disagree: they argue that euthanasia could still be morally acceptable on Kantian grounds.

> IF WE ALLOW JUST A FEW VERY ILL PEOPLE IN PAIN TO CHOOSE EUTHANASIA, THIS WOULDN'T DESTROY THE CONCEPT OF "EUTHANASIA" OR "LIFE" IN EVERYONE'S MIND, AS KANT CLAIMS.

> SO IT WOULDN'T BE "IRRATIONAL" OR IMMORAL TO ALLOW IT IN A FEW RARE INSTANCES.

The Utilitarians

John Stuart Mill also stressed the importance of allowing individuals
the freedom to choose what to do with their lives, provided no-one
else suffered as a result. The "liberty argument" is a very strong one
for Utilitarians.

Utilitarians do seem to offer the most help in clarifying, if not solving, the
problem of euthanasia. Utilitarians would think very carefully about the
consequences of euthanasia for the patient, his relatives and friends,
the medical profession and its reputation amongst the general public.

A Utilitarian doctor who decided whether or not to allow euthanasia would be entering dangerous territory.

Imagine the difficulties faced by a Utilitarian doctor having to say to someone who is in great pain …

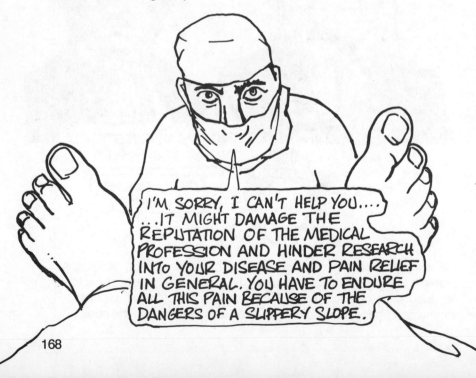

Virtue Theory Again

Euthanasia is a good case for "virtue theory" and how it might help us to make moral decisions. It is because of the apparently conflicting advice offered to us by Utilitarians and Kantians in situations like these that some philosophers suggest that euthanasia just isn't "solvable" by appealing to ethical "systems".

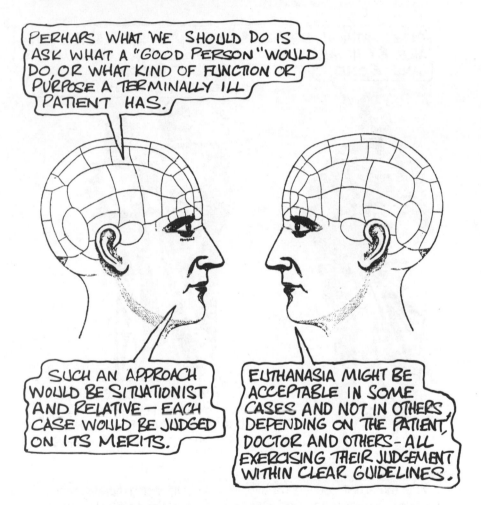

PERHAPS WHAT WE SHOULD DO IS ASK WHAT A "GOOD PERSON" WOULD DO, OR WHAT KIND OF FUNCTION OR PURPOSE A TERMINALLY ILL PATIENT HAS.

SUCH AN APPROACH WOULD BE SITUATIONIST AND RELATIVE — EACH CASE WOULD BE JUDGED ON ITS MERITS.

EUTHANASIA MIGHT BE ACCEPTABLE IN SOME CASES AND NOT IN OTHERS, DEPENDING ON THE PATIENT, DOCTOR AND OTHERS — ALL EXERCISING THEIR JUDGEMENT WITHIN CLEAR GUIDELINES.

How the law could enter such arrangements, though, is hard to envisage, which makes some Aristotelians suggest that perhaps euthanasia is simply not something the law should get involved with at all. One wonders what Dr Cox might say.

What Do We Conclude?

Ethics is difficult and probably always will be. It may derive partly
from human nature – even if much of that is merely a useful fiction.
Usually the attempt has been to make ethics objective and universal,
when the evidence is clear that there is a huge range of different
beliefs about how we should behave towards each other.

OLDER ETHICAL DOCTRINES ARE BY NO MEANS DEAD AND GONE.

SOME PHILOSOPHERS STILL BELIEVE THAT MORALITY IS ABOUT PRODUCING AND DISTRIBUTING HAPPINESS.

AND UTILITARIANISM STILL SEEMS A HELPFUL SYSTEM FOR ANALYZING AND EVALUATING (IF NOT SOLVING) COMPLEX PRACTICAL MORAL PROBLEMS.

Other moral philosophers believe, like Kant, that being moral means
acting rationally and consistently. The return of "virtue ethics" may help
to avoid some of the undesirable consequences of these other two
doctrines but can itself be embarrassingly vague about how
"situationally sensitive" individuals make moral decisions which are
consistent and committed.

Postmodernism has accelerated our epistemological crisis. It is difficult now to be confident about the certainty of any human knowledge, especially knowledge about human beings themselves. It seems very unlikely that we shall ever discover universal and objective moral truths. The discovery of such truths looks even less likely than a discovery of what was around before the Big Bang.

THE BELIEF THAT HUMBLE PRIMATES COULD EVER DISCOVER SUCH METAPHYSICAL ENTITIES NOW LOOKS ARROGANT, DANGEROUS AND RATHER ODD.

BUT THIS INFORMED SCEPTICISM CAN BE A POSITIVE THING.

IT SHOULD MAKE US SUSPICIOUS OF CHARISMATIC GURUS, INFLAMMATORY POLITICAL LEADERS AND ALL THOSE WHO CLAIM TO HAVE A HOTLINE TO THE MORAL TRUTH.

Because we can only make small tentative steps towards some form of limited and subjective human moral progress doesn't mean that such a thing is impossible.

As a species we have been, and still are, wonderfully inventive, creative and adventurous. But in spite of our microwave ovens and computers, we are still at a very primitive stage of moral development. Postmodernism may well have destroyed ethical certainty, but paradoxically it is this destruction that may help us to make moral progress.

This may mean that we end up living in smaller, ethically autonomous "tribes", or larger societies which are healthily pluralist and "open".

An idea known as the **"Anthropic Principle"** has been developed by recent cosmologists. This Principle looks at "possible" universes and proposes that our universe was specifically structured to allow human life to evolve successfully. If that's true, then we humans have been incredibly lucky to survive against almost impossible universal odds.

If we can face the fact that we are merely human beings with a limited grasp of a "knowledge", which we get via an unreliable set of human perceptual and conceptual equipment, then there may be hope for us. We can never achieve ethical certainty. But we can become more morally aware. If, as a species, we don't, then we just won't make it.

Ethics is still definitely something worth going in for.

FURTHER READING

There are rather a lot of books on ethics. This book has referred to these texts directly:
Plato's **Republic**; K. Popper's **The Open Society and Its Enemies**; Aristotle's **Nichomachean Ethics**; Hobbes' **Leviathan**; Rousseau's **Emile**; Machiavelli's **The Prince**; John Stuart Mill's **Utilitarianism** and **On Liberty**; Kant's **The Moral Law**; Hume's **A Treatise of Human Nature**; A.J. Ayer's **Language, Truth and Logic**; R. Hare's **The Language of Morals**; J.-P. Sartre's **Existentialism and Humanism**; J. Rawls' **A Theory of Social Justice**; A. MacIntyre's **After Virtue**; M. Nussbaum's **Love's Knowledge**; Z. Bauman's **Intimations of Postmodernity**.

Good general introductory books on ethics that are very useful are:
The Puzzle of Ethics, Paul Vardy and Paul Grosch (Harper-Collins 1994); **Moral Philosophy**, D.D. Raphael (Oxford 1981); **Moral Principles and Social Values**, J. Trusted (Routledge 1987); **A Short History of Ethics**, A. MacIntyre (Routledge 1967); **Ethics**, J.L. Mackie (Penguin 1977).

A book which is not "philosophical" but very interesting is:
Seven Theories of Human Nature, L. Stevenson (Oxford 1974).

There are many books on the Greek philosophers, like: **Plato**, Nickolas Pappas (Routledge 1995); **Plato's Republic**, R. Cross and A.D. Woozley (Macmillan 1979); **Aristotle the Philosopher**, J. Ackrill (Oxford 1981); **Aristotle's Ethics**, J. Urmson (Blackwell 1988); **Aristotle's Ethical Theory**, W. Hardie (Oxford 1981).
Two shorter introductions for those with less time are:
Plato, R. Hare (Oxford Past Masters 1984); **Aristotle**, J. Barnes (Oxford Past Masters 1982).

A good introduction to Mill, Kant and Sartre is:
Three Philosophical Moralists, G. Kerner (Oxford 1990).

The shortest and often clearest guide to Kant's moral philosophy is still **Kant's Moral Philosophy**, H.B. Acton (Macmillan 1970).
Another very clear book is **An Introduction to Kant's Ethics**, R. Sullivan (Cambridge 1994).

Clear but not always simple introductions to more theoretical modern moral philosophy are: **Modern Moral Philosophy**, W.D. Hudson (Macmillan 1983); **Contemporary Moral Philosophy**, G.J. Warnock (Macmillan 1967).

Good introductions to applied ethics from a generally Utilitarian standpoint are: **Practical Ethics**, P. Singer (Oxford 1993); **Applied Ethics**, ed. P. Singer (Oxford 1986).

A good dialectical introduction to Utilitarian Philosophy is **Utilitarianism: For and Against**, J.J. Smart and B. Williams (Cambridge 1973). The most thorough and fascinating introduction to political philosophy can be found in the two volumes of **Man and Society**, J. Plamenatz (Longman 1992); a shorter but interesting introduction is in the essays contained in **Political Ideas**, ed. D. Thomson (Penguin 1990).

A clear account of more recent moral and political theory is in: **Modern Political Philosophy**, A. Brown (Penguin 1986); **Political Thinkers**, ed. D. Muschamp (Macmillan 1986); **Public and Private Morality**, ed. S. Hampshire (Cambridge 1978).

Other books on practical ethics are: **Animals and Why They Matter**, M. Midgley (Penguin 1983); **Animal Liberation**, P. Singer (Cape 1976); **Causing Death and Saving Lives**, J. Glover (Penguin 1972).

The most recent and very good collection of essays on all manner of historical, theoretical and practical ethical subjects is: **A Companion to Ethics**, ed. P. Singer (Blackwell 1993).

Philosophy Now is an excellent, unstuffy and accessible magazine that comes out quarterly and often covers contemporary moral issues. It is obtainable from 226 Bramford Road, Ipswich IP1 4AS.

Acknowledgements

I'd like to mention **A Companion to Ethics** as especially useful to this author, although, unsurprisingly, I haven't agreed with every single view expressed in that anthology. I'd also like to thank the unnatural patience shown me by my companion Judith and all those friends I forced to read my original manuscript. I'm always grateful to my students for making me laugh and providing me with some of the very few original ideas in this book. I am also full of admiration for Chris Garratt who has made this book more fun than it might have been. Thanks also to my editor, Richard Appignanesi, who had to remind me patiently what commas are for. Finally I would like to thank Professor R.F. Atkinson for much of my formal and informal education in ethical philosophy. I would recommend everyone read his book **Conduct: An Introduction to Moral Philosophy** (Macmillan 1969) when they have finished with this one.

Artwork assistants
Diane Dalton
Sophie Garratt
Duncan Heath

Index